Holzman on Hoops

Holzman on Hoops

The Man Who Led
The Knicks Through Two
World Championships
Tells It Like It Was

Red Holzman
and Harvey Frommer

Taylor Publishing Company
Dallas, Texas

Published by Taylor Publishing Company
1550 West Mockingbird Lane
Dallas, Texas 75235

Photographs courtesy of The Basketball Hall of Fame

Designed by David Timmons Graphic Design

Library of Congress Cataloging-in-Publication Data

Holzman, Red.
    Holzman on hoops : the man who led the Knicks through two world
championships tells it like it was / Red Holzman with Harvey
Frommer.
        p.   cm.
    Includes index.
    ISBN 0-87833-745-8 : $18.95
    1. Basketball—United States—History. 2. New York Knickerbockers
(Basketball team)—History. 3. Basketball—United States—
Miscellanea. I. Frommer, Harvey. II. Title.
GV885.7.H65   1991
796.323′0973—dc20   91-15154
                                                                    CIP

Printed in the United States of America

10 9 8 7 6 5 4 3 2 1

*To Selma, Gail, and the
guys who gave 1,000 percent
every night*

Acknowledgments

n opus like this could never have been possible without a lot of helping hands, piercing eyes, and willing spirits. I would like to thank all of them right here in this space.

At the very top of the list is my wife Selma Holzman. She coined the book's title, listened to the words, and gave us all inspiration. A tip of my hat goes also to my daughter Gail.

I made my co-author Harvey Frommer my number-one draft choice for my autobiography *Red on Red*. He did a great job there. Now, against all odds, he's proved himself again with another great job. A lot of the categories for this book were his invention. If you don't like them—give him the blame. If you like them—give us both credit.

Myrna Frommer was of invaluable assistance, and the Frommer team on the bench— Jennifer, Freddy, and Ian—also helped in getting this tome tuned up.

Agent Artie Pine made the deal. Lou Wolfe was there for the opening tap, but our editor, Jim Donovan, picked up the dribble and scored the winning basket.

All the good people at the Basketball Hall of Fame in Springfield gave us a lot to work with. Wayne Patterson (who cheerfully and competently supplies most of the photos and great archival material), Joe O'Brien, Jerry Healy—a special thanks to all of you.

The NBA Office and Brian McIntyre, Terry Lyons, Jim Harter, and Alex Sachare are owed a huge debt for making "NBA News" available to us. And Fuzzy Levane . . . what can I say? Thanks, buddy.

Others who make the acknowledgment list include: Roz Puretz, Ceil Kolber, Harry Kolber, Ira Berkow, Red Phillips, Les Harrison, David Stern, Red Sarachek, Len Lewin, Richard Evans, Jack Diller, John Cirillo, George Kalinsky, Teddy Leb, Herb Gershon, Henry Gershon, Pickles Banks, Joel Berger, Roy Cravzow, and Billy Feigenbaum.

Contents

Twenty-four pages of photographs follow page 86

Introduction

ontrary to all the rumors you might have heard, I wasn't the guy in the balcony holding the nail when James Naismith hammered up the peach basket to start what we all know and love—basketball, America's game. But I've been around hoops for a long time, a long, long time.

Mine has been a real basketball life. It seems all I've really ever done professionally has been with the sport. I've been an active part of professional basketball since 1945, probably longer than anyone else around. I've seen the game grow and change. Teams that once were there are no more, and other teams have come along and replaced them. Players that have been called the greatest ever have come and gone. And others who have been called the greatest ever have come along and replaced them.

Whenever I talk or write about what once was and is now, I'm reminded of the famous exchange between a pretty old Casey Stengel and a pretty young Mickey Mantle.

"You once played baseball, Casey?" Mickey asked.

"What the hell, do you think I was born as an old man right here on the Yankee bench? Sure I played."

I played, too. My autobiography, *Red on Red* (I figured I'd get a plug in for that), goes into a lot of detail about me. This book is about others, but once in a while, I'll get myself into it.

Here's a "once in a while." I played three years in the National Basketball League; twice I was a first team All-Star. Then, in 1948-49 (when Kareem Abdul-Jabbar was just one year old), my Rochester Royals team and three other clubs jumped from the National Basketball League into the Basketball Association of America—the league that was to become the NBA. For you trivia buffs, the three other teams that came over to the BAA with Rochester were the Minneapolis Lakers, the Fort Wayne Pistons, and the Indianapolis Jets. The BAA had two divisions. The Eastern Division had the Washington Capitols (coached by Red Auerbach), the New York Knickerbockers, the Baltimore Bullets, the Philadelphia Warriors, and the Providence Steamrollers. The Western Division had the St. Louis Bombers and Chicago Gears plus the four former NBL teams.

How long ago was that 1948-49 season? Well, the Minneapolis Lakers with George Mikan leading the way defeated Washington to win the championship on April 15. Today, the NBA season is just winding down on that date. George played in that series with a busted-up and bandaged wrist. After the series, he and another guy from Minnesota met at the White House. The other guy autographed George's wrist bandage. The guy's name was Senator Hubert H. Humphrey. I wonder if George still has that autographed bandage.

Some perspective on how the game has changed from then till now: only three guys averaged twenty or more points a game that first sixty-game season, and Bob Davies, my Rochester teammate, led the league in assists with 5.4 a game.

I get kind of nostalgic when I think of Bob Davies and other teammates on the Rochester Royals: Bobby Wanzer, Al Cervi, Fuzzy Levane, and my old coach Lester Harrison. Playing basketball in Rochester was a joy. Before that, making all-American at City College with Nat Holman as my coach, being a kid on a New York City Workmen's Circle team coached by Red Sarachek—those were joyful times, too. I also played for Local 102 in New York, a team coached by Marty Cohen. We had players like Herb Gershon, Pickles Banks, and Leo Gottlieb. As a player, I was in more one-night stands all across little cities and big towns throughout America than I'd like to remember. Then, as a scout and as a coach, I made more stops than a Greyhound bus driver earning a commission for miles covered.

I've been lauded, conned, hustled, hired, fired, enshrined, faked out, rained on, impressed, depressed, involved, detached, thrilled, saddened, bored, and turned on. I've seen it all in my basketball life. I've been around the game of hoops for more than fifty years. It's a game I love. In the pages of this opus, a book about basketball, I'll kid you, kid you again, quiz you, inform you, and stagger you with history, data, stats, and insight—just like my agent, Artie Pine, said I would.

Like Alfred Hitchcock in his movies, I'm going to

pop in and pop out of different parts of this book to put my personal touch on all the stuff I'll be presenting.

Holzman On Hoops is going to be a little like my wife Selma's vegetable soup: a bit of this and a bit of that. But her soup is great stuff. It fills you up, and you always want to come back for more next time. I want this book to fill you up with a hefty helping of hoop stuff. Then maybe you'll come back for the sequel.

1

The Early Years

asketball today is a sport played all over the world, and every year it gets more and more popular. But its popularity is not a new thing. Even before World War II, it was pretty big worldwide, with more than seventy-five countries playing the game. The advertising slogan "America's Game" is not just an advertising slogan—it's true. Basketball is the only sport invented in the United States that does not have its roots in a foreign sport. It's strange to think that the game began way back in 1891—that was even before my time.

Back then Dr. James Naismith, a phys ed instructor at the international YMCA Training School in Springfield, Massachusetts, was told by his chairman to think up some kind of game for his students to fill the time between fall football and spring baseball. The Canadian-born Naismith was also told that the game had to be played indoors—it seemed that the students balked at the idea of going outdoors in the cold to play ball. They must have been a bunch of sissies.

Naismith figured that only a game with a ball and goals would be practical. He began tinkering around with versions of soccer, lacrosse, and rugby, trying to adapt those sports to indoor play. Once a few windows were broken and a few players got some bumps and bruises, it was clear that idea wasn't going to work. Then Naismith decided to develop a non-contact type of game, a game that didn't allow the players to run with the ball.

As the story goes, Naismith decided that he would use a soccer ball and some boxes as goals for his game. Naismith said later, "As I walked down the hall, I met Mr. Stebbins, the superintendent of buildings. I asked him if he had two boxes about eighteen inches square."

"No, I haven't any boxes," was the superintendent's reply, "But I have two old peach baskets in the storeroom. You think those will do you any good?"

"Bring them up," Naismith told the super. "We'll try them."

The superintendent brought up the baskets and Naismith went to work with a hammer and a couple of nails. The baskets were nailed up to the lower rail of the balconies at each end of the gym. Since the spot the baskets were nailed up to was ten feet above the ground, that became the standard height for a basket. Then Naismith scribbled out his thirteen rules for the new game on a pad. The notes were deciphered by the school secretary, typed out on two sheets of paper, and tacked up on the bulletin board outside the gym entrance. A while later these original rules appeared in the school newspaper under the headline A NEW GAME.

Even though the rules are a bit wordy and dated, they have a lot of charm. And since they formed the basis for the game of basketball, I decided to include them here as Naismith passed them on to posterity. You can pass over the next few paragraphs, though, if you get bored with that kind of thing.

"The goals are a couple of baskets or boxes about fifteen inches diameter across the opening, and about fifteen inches deep. These are suspended, one at each end of the grounds, about ten feet from the floor. The object of the game is to put the ball into your opponent's goal. This may be done from throwing the ball from any part of the grounds with one or both hands, under the following conditions and rules:

"The ball to be an ordinary Association football (soccer ball).

" 1. The ball may be thrown in any direction with one or both hands.

" 2. The ball may be batted in any direction with one or both hands (never with the fist).

" 3. A player can not run with the ball. The player must throw it from the spot on which he catches it, allowance to be made for a man who catches the ball while running at a good speed if he tries to stop.

" 4. The ball must be held in or between the hands. The arms or body must not be used for holding it.

" 5. No shouldering, holding, pushing, tripping or striking in any way the person of any opponent shall be allowed; the first infringement of this rule by any player shall count as a foul, the second shall disqualify him until the next goal is made, or, if there was evident intent to injure the person, for the whole of the game, no substitute allowed.

" 6. A foul is striking at the ball with the fist, violation of Rules 3, 4, and such as described in Rule 5.

" 7. If either side makes three consecutive fouls, it shall count a goal for the opponents (consecutive means without the opponents in the meantime making a foul).

" 8. A goal shall be made when the ball is thrown or batted from the ground into the basket and stays there providing those defending the goal do not disturb the goal. If the ball rests on the edges and the opponents move the basket, it shall count as a goal.

" 9. When the ball goes out of bounds it shall be thrown into the field of play by the first person touching it. In case of a dispute, the umpire shall throw it straight into the field. The thrower-in is allowed five seconds, if he holds it longer, it shall go to an opponent. If any side persists in delaying the game, the umpire shall call a foul on that side.

"10. The umpire shall be judge of the men and shall note the fouls and notify the referee when three consecutive fouls have been made. He shall have power to disqualify men according to Rule 5.

"11. The referee shall be judge of the ball and shall decide when the ball is in play, in bounds, to which side it belongs, and shall keep time. He shall decide when a goal has been made, and keep account of the goals with any other duties that are usually performed by the referee.

"12. The time shall be fifteen minute halves, with five minutes rest between.

"13. The side making the most goals in that time shall be declared the winner. In case of a draw, the game may, by agreement of the captains, be continued until another goal is made.

"The number composing a team depends largely on the size of the floor space, but it may range from three on a side to forty. The fewer players down to three, the more scientific it may be made, but the more players, the more fun. The men may be arranged according to the idea of the captain, but it has been found that a goal keeper, two guards, three center men, two wings, and a home man stationed in the above order from the goal is the best.

"It shall be the duty of the goal keeper and the two guards to prevent the opponents from scoring. The duty of the wing men and the home man is to put the ball into the opponent's goal, and the center men shall feed the ball forward to the man who has the best opportunity, thus nine men make the best number for a team."

Although some might have said that a Philadelphia lawyer was needed to decipher all the options on those rules, those rules formed the basis of the new game. They still do. The first five rules set Naismith's game apart from all other ball games, especially all those games that involved physical contact. Key parts of the Naismith game allowed players to throw the ball in any direction but banned them from striking it with their fists, holding the ball against their bodies, running with the ball. All rough stuff was banned; it was supposed to be a non-contact sport. That's how all the fouls and penalties were immediately a part of the game. Three team fouls between goals counted as a goal. A player committing a second foul was banished to the sidelines until the next goal was scored. Any player trying to deliberately hurt another player was disqualified from a game with no subbing allowed for him.

A lot of people suggested that the new game be called "Naismith Ball" but the good doctor was too modest. "That name," he smiled, "would kill any game." Instead the name "basket ball" was used for the game he invented—after the peach baskets that were used. Two words—basket ball—was the name of the game until

1921, when they were combined into the one word that everyone uses today. Maybe it's a good thing that the superintendent couldn't find the boxes Naismith wanted, or else the sport would've probably been called box ball. And then the kids on my block when I was growing up in Brooklyn would've had to come up with a new name for the game we played that *was* called box ball.

When the first member of Naismith's class arrived and read the rules that were tacked up on the bulletin board and looked at the peach baskets hanging there, the kid was not too impressed. "Huh," he groaned. "Another new game."

But he played in that first game in December of 1891. There were nine players on a side—only because eighteen students happened to show up. James Naismith, the inventor of the sport, was also its first coach and first ref. He blew his whistle many times and kept shouting, "Pass it! Pass it! Pass the ball!" Sound familiar? The only basket in that first game was scored by William R. Chase of New Bedford, Massachusetts. And I guess that 1-0 score still stands as the lowest score in a basketball game ever.

I'm being kind of charitable calling it a basketball game. What it was more like was primitive basketball. At first they used a ladder to get the ball out of the peach basket. Then the kids sitting in the balconies were given jobs—to take the ball out of the basket after a score.

Things really got sophisticated when someone came up with the idea of drilling a hole in the bottom of the peach basket. A long pole was used to punch up through the hole to get the ball out.

Teamwork belonged to the future. It was kind of like every man for himself at the start; guys would whack away at each other and the ball. At times more than half a team would be on the sidelines in the penalty area. There were a whole lot of guys out there playing on a small floor thirty-five by fifty feet. A lot of shots went up but only a few of them went in. They weren't very big on shooting percentages in those days.

But as Naismith wrote, "The game was a success from the time the first ball was tossed up. The players were interested in and seemed to enjoy the game. Word soon got around that they were having fun in Naismith's gym class."

Naismith really got the ball rolling and on record when the Springfield school he taught at printed the rules of his new game in *The Triangle,* the school magazine, on January 15, 1892. Then students and teachers at the school took part in what has gone down in history as the first "public played" game of basketball. The date was March 11, 1892. I guess the students were in better shape because they wound up beating the teachers, 5-1. They probably also had more fans in the crowd of 200 that watched the game. But let the record also note that the only goal scored by the teachers was recorded by Amos Alonzo Stagg—now that's a familiar name.

That year of 1892 the sport of basket ball as it was then known was introduced in Mexico and began its adventure as a worldwide American export.

As the game was played, it changed and evolved. The original idea of Naismith's that "any number could play" never did work out well even though some tried it. At Cornell University, a guy named Ed Hitchcock introduced the game to his class of a hundred students. With fifty players on a side, it wasn't a game—it was a mob scene. Smaller mob scenes took place in games with twenty on a team, eight on a team. It wasn't until 1897 that five guys on a side became standard.

In 1894, the free throw was introduced. Each team was allowed to have a specialist who did its foul shooting. That practice stayed in effect until 1924. The first guys shot free throws from twenty feet out.

Those old rickety peach baskets were replaced almost immediately by metal baskets. In 1892, Lee Allen of Hartford, Connecticut, came up with the idea of cylindrical baskets of heavy woven wire with a chain pull to drop the ball out. One year later the Narragansett Machine Company of Providence, Rhode Island, did Lee Allen one better. It started to manufacture baskets with iron rims and braided cord netting.

In 1894, the soccer balls that were used for basket ball were replaced by an official basketball. Those first basketballs, just a bit larger than the original soccer balls, were made by a bike manufacturer—the Overman Wheel Company of Chicopee Falls, Massachusetts. In the late 1890s Spalding took over as the company making the balls. And other companies have had that honor since: MacGregor, Wilson, Rawlings, Voit, etc. Through the years the size of the ball has been changed many times. There was a time when the ball was 32 inches around with a weight of 23 ounces. Today the ball can't weigh more than 22 ounces or less than 20 ounces and the circumference has to be between $29\frac{1}{2}$ and 30 inches.

At one time, field goals and foul shots both counted three points each. In the season of 1895–96 the standard two points for a field goal and one point for a foul shot came into vogue, and it was that way all along until the three-point shot was adopted in the ABA and then the NBA.

In 1906, open metal hoops similar to the kind used today were introduced. But that setup wasn't approved for use by amateurs until 1912.

Backboards were put up almost at the beginning to keep fans out of the action and away from batting the ball. The first backboards were heavy wire mesh. Then in 1895–96 a 6′ × 4′ wooden backboard became standard. The backboard got a nice white paint job in 1906–07.

It was kind of tough, though, for the fans sitting behind those wooden backboards to see what the hell was going on, but it wasn't until 1909–10 that somebody's bright idea of a plate-glass backboard was first approved in the rules. As everyone knows who has sat behind the glass backboard, you can't beat the view.

Other big rule changes in those early years that shaped the game included: banning the "air dribble" and "double dribble" in 1898. It took a couple of years, but by 1900, the one-hand dribble was a tactic used by almost everyone.

Ironically, during my growing-up years, I got to see the "two-hand dribble" as part of the big basketball action of the time. It was one of the special features of play in the American League, a league that lasted from 1926 to 1946. That was a pro league that had teams in Washington, Trenton, Philadelphia, New York, Cleveland, Ft. Wayne, Detroit, and Chicago. Some pretty heavy hitters were also owners in that league: George Halas, the guy who also owned the Chicago Bears, "Slapsie Maxie" Rosenbloom, who made his name in boxing, and George Preston Marshall, who owned the Washington Redskins football team.

My uncle often took me to Arcadia Hall in the Bushwick section of Brooklyn to watch the Jewels play basketball. They were a bunch of guys that had been known in college as the St. John's Wonder Five, then had played together as pros in the American Basketball League. The star of that team was Mac Kinsbrunner, a super dribbler, a guy who was able to control the ball all night long if he had to.

Games in the ABL were divided into fifteen-minute thirds, not halves. There was very little motion in the game. A player was not allowed to shoot with his back to the basket and no screening or blocking was allowed. If a guy did that, his team lost the ball. But probably the most unusual feature of the game was the·two-hand-dribble— that same dribble that had been banned in 1898 but had found new life in the ABL. The only way a player could dribble was forward. If he went backwards he would lose the ball. It was something to see Mac Kinsbrunner dribble that basketball with two hands and going forward all the time. It had such an impression on me that for weeks after I saw him play I would be out there in the schoolyard dribbling that basketball with two hands and pretending to be the great Mac Kinsbrunner daring guys to try to steal the ball off me.

From the start James Naismith had a hunch that basketball would be a good game for women to play. It was actually the first active sport played by women. Naismith organized the first women's game in Springfield in 1892 and got a big bonus out of that organizing. He married one of the players who competed in that game—a young woman named Maude Sherman.

On March 22, 1893, Smith College in Northampton, Massachusetts, became the first women's school to play basketball. The women were a little fussy about who they allowed in to watch them. All men were barred from attending the goings on.

There were a few men around, though, to see one of the first women's basketball games on the intercollegiate level—on April 4, 1895, when California played Stanford. A year before that game Smith College had a team organized by Sendra Berenson, who was the director of physical education there. The women's basketball game had a set of rules designed to make the game a gentler one than the one the men played. The floor was divided into three sections and females playing the game had to remain in their zone the whole game. They also were limited to two or three bounces per dribble. Women were banned from snatching the ball out of the hands of another player. After a while not all the women went along with this approach that made for a kind of dull and static game. More and more women began to play the game according to men's rules, and by 1914, about half the women's basketball played in the United States was played according to men's rules.

One of the greatest success stories in women's basketball is the record of the Edmonton Grads, alumnae of the John A. McDougall Commercial High School of Edmonton in Alberta, Canada. From 1915 to 1940 that team won 502 games, losing only 20. And some of their games were against men's teams. They had a streak in there of 78 straight wins.

Although the roughness in basketball was at one time only a pet peeve and complaint of women educators, the YMCAs got kind of alarmed at all the pushing and shoving that was taking place in the game. For a non-contact sport there was too much contact.

But that didn't keep the game from growing. A lot of the growth was stimulated by Naismith, the inventor of the game, who turned into one of its big early promoters. In 1892, he organized a team that went on a tour of the East. That same year he set up games between two YMCAs and two women's teams. YMCA tournaments sprang up all over the place. In 1897, a tourney was played for the national championship. It wasn't that national, though. Most of the teams came from New York City. The 23rd Street YMCA won the first Amateur Athletic Union National Championship in a game played on its own home court.

The first game with five-man teams was played between the University of Chicago and the University of Iowa on January 16, 1896. The game, played in Iowa City, turned out to be a real basketball happening. Excitement built for that grand event for weeks. Store windows had all kinds of displays advertising the game. And as a special feature the debating clubs of both universities went at it a couple of days before the big game. Chicago wound up winning the game, 15-12. One Iowa newspaper had a story afterwards that said: "The strict officiating was a source of great dissatisfaction to the audience."

Even back then refs were given a hard time.

As the nineteenth century ended YMCA basketball was beginning to get more and more rugged. There was violence and a kind of "win at any cost" mentality all over the place. Part of the roughness came from Rule Number 9, that dealt with the first player touching the ball getting possession of it when it went out of bounds. That rule led to mayhem—guys clobbering each other to get possession of the ball.

There were meetings, editorials in newspapers, special hearings, all aimed at doing something about the problem. What was done was kind of drastic. All Philadelphia YMCAs dropped the sport and lots of basketball programs were dropped in other Eastern cities, too.

Those moves didn't kill the sport. Instead, guys who had played it in Y's and were now forced out of the Y's simply organized teams of their own. They rented space where they could play and charged admission to pay the rent. And that was how pro basketball began—primitive, but pro basketball.

One report of the first professional basketball game says it took place in 1893 in Herkimer, New York. But that's just one report. Most of the experts agree that the first professional game took place in 1896 in Trenton, New Jersey, in a Masonic Temple Auditorium. Two top players on that Trenton team were Fred Cooper, the captain, and Albert Bratton, both skilled soccer players. They knew how to pass the ball from their soccer training. There was such a mob at the game that after expenses there was money left over so that each Trenton player got fifteen bucks. The captain of the team, Cooper, who had more pull, received sixteen dollars.

By 1898 the first pro league was in action—the National Basketball League. The six charter members included: Trenton, New Jersey; Camden, New Jersey; Millville, Pennsylvania; the Pennsylvania Bike Club of Philadelphia; the Hancock Athletic Club; and the Germantown Club. Other leagues started popping up all over the East. Most of the games took place on dance floors. Chicken-coop fencing kept the fans off the playing floor. The whole spectacle looked like guys playing in a cage—and that's how the nickname "cagers" for basketball players, and the "cage" game for the sport came into being.

At the start, pro basketball was a pick-up affair. Guys played for the best price and sometimes played for several different teams in several different leagues. One of the early legendary teams was the Buffalo Germans, originally a YMCA team of fourteen-year-olds organized in 1895.

The Pan-American Exposition was staged in Buffalo in 1901 and part of it included a basketball tournament. It must have been something to see because the games were played on a 40′ × 60′ grass court and players all wore cleats. That didn't bother the Buffalo Germans any. They beat all the competition in the preliminary games, but their fans were a bit shaken as the final game started. It turned out that some of the Germans' players were missing, so they started the game with only three men. After seven minutes of the game had elapsed one of the missing Germans came onto the court. That was only after he found parking space for his bike. A couple of minutes later another star player arrived—in street clothes. He played the rest of that first half that way. It didn't hurt him or Buffalo any. The Germans would up winning the game 10-1. Those games back then were real defensive struggles.

At that same Pan-American Exposition a competition was staged that was called "the national high school basketball tournament." Holyoke (Massachusetts) High School won the championship by trimming Mt. Vernon, New York, and Pratt Institute of New York.

The first college conference was created during that 1901–02 season. It was called the Triangular League and was composed of Yale, Trinity, and Wesleyan. A New England League quickly followed, with teams from Amherst, Williams, Dartmouth, Trinity, and Holy Cross.

In 1904, in the Olympics in St. Louis, the Buffalo Germans won the first Olympic basketball demonstration tournament and turned pro the next year. As part of that Olympiad a national college tourney was staged outdoors as an exhibition. Hiram College used a victory over Latter Day Saints University (we know the place today as Brigham Young University) to win the entire tournament.

Hiram College didn't accomplish too much after that in the world of basketball, but one of the Buffalo Germans, "Phog" Allen, did. A guy who had played and coached for the Buffalo Germans, Allen succeeded Dr. Naismith as head coach at Kansas University. His first game was on December 13, 1907—a 66-22 rout of Ottawa. "Phog" Allen became one of the legends of the game. His teams won 771 games and 31 championships in 39 seasons.

Allen kept rolling along and so did the Buffalo Germans. In a thirty-year span the Germans played any team in any place at any time and wound up winning 792 games against just 86 losses. They had a string of 111 straight wins. Two guys, Eddie Miller and Al Heerdt, were on the Germans from the time the team began to the day it ended. In 1931, the Germans staged a comeback for one last game, an exhibition game. They won it. The average age of the players on that team then was fifty-one years old.

One of the great pro players of that era was a tiny guy named Barney Sedran. Later, he was my coach in 1945, when I kind of moonlighted as a basketball player with Troy, New York. Barney is in the Hall of Fame and he belongs there. I can still see him in my mind's eye smoking that cigar and telling the old stories.

Barney was only 5'4" and 118 pounds in his prime. They thought he was too small to play basketball at De-Witt Clinton High School in New York City, but he went on to star for City College of New York. Three years in a row he led the team in scoring and then went on to play pro ball for fifteen years. Some of his glory days were with the New York Whirlwinds, a team he played on with

Nat Holman, another legend. That gave that team two great guards—two excellent little men who at different times coached me. Nat was my coach when I played for City College.

With Utica, New York, in the 1913–14 season, Barney once scored in double figures in a game. You say, so what? Well, he did that shooting at a basket without a backboard and getting pounded by guys with blood in their eyes.

"In those days," Barney told me, "I kept playing. If you left a game you were out and you weren't allowed back in. Players were always thrown against the chicken wire that surrounded the court. Many of us were cut several times. And the court was usually covered with blood.

"A sign of a pro basketball player in those days was a broken nose. I bet," Barney smiled, "that about ninety percent of the guys that played had broken noses. Those games were more like hockey games than basketball. It was rough."

Probably the first great pro team was the Celtics. They started out in 1914 as the New York Celtics, a group of guys that played together representing the Henry Street settlement house. After World War I, they were reorganized by boxing promoter Tex Ricard and called the Original Celtics.

Standout players on the Original Celtics through the years included 6'5" Joe Lapchick, one of the games's first "big men"; Johnny Beckman, the "designated foul shooter" in an era when one guy did all the foul shooting for his team, Pete Barry, Ernie Reich, Nat Holman, Dave Banks, Chris Leonard, George Haggerty, Dutch Dehnert, Elmer Ripley, Harry Brugge, Benny Borgmann, "Stretch" Meehan, Jim Kane, and "Chief" Mueller. A lot of those guys went on to become fabled figures in basketball—college coaches, experts on the game—and many of them are in the Basketball Hall of Fame.

The Celtics were probably the first team to be in business as a unit with none of their guys moonlighting with other teams. You played for the Celtics—and nobody else. Their style of play put a premium on team basketball. The Celtics played a switching and aggressive one-on-one defense. The give-and-go was invented by the Celtics, and so was pivot play.

Actually, pivot play was accidentally invented by Dutch Dehnert. Back in those days it was the thing for a team to have what was called a "standing guard," a guy who stayed at the defensive foul line at all times. Dutch would stand with his back to the guard, getting set to receive a pass. After the pass, when the guard tried to move around him to get his hands on the ball, Dutch would pivot in the other direction and go for a layup or pass the ball to one of his teammates cutting past him.

A three-game series between the Celtics and the New York Whirlwinds (who had Nat Holman) in 1921 wound up making the Celtics an even stronger team, and according to Nat Holman "broke up what I always thought was the greatest team of all time—the Whirlwinds."

The first game between the two teams was played before 11,000 fans at the 71st Regiment Armory in New York City. That one went to the Whirlwinds, 40-27. The next game was at the 69th Regiment Armory; the Celtics won by two points. There was never a third game. I guess both teams had their pride. When that '21 season ended, both Nat Holman and Chris Leonard were signed up by the Celtics. "The offer amounted to more than we had ever dreamed of making playing ball. We couldn't turn it down," Nat Holman told me.

In the 1922–23 season the Celtics also added Joe Lapchick. Joe starred for the Celtics for a decade and then moved on to a great career as a coach for St. John's University. With Lapchick and Holman and the others doing their thing the Celtics were the best team of their time in all of pro basketball.

They loved being an independent team and playing anybody, anyplace, anytime, and getting those big pay-days. But the American League forced the Celtics to become part of their operation. The Celtics were told that none of the American Basketball League teams would play them unless they joined the league.

It was a painful but easy decision for the Celtics—join up or lose out on playing against basketball's top teams. They joined up.

The Celtics became a member of the American Basketball League that was created in 1925 and were the class of that operation, winning the championship two straight years. In the 1927–28 season they won 109 out of 120 games played. First the ABL wooed the Celtics, then they wound up hating them because of their talent.

"Break up the Celtics" was the chant. And the next year they were actually broken up and shipped around the ABL. Joe Lapchick, Pete Barry, and Dutch Dehnert wound up with the Cleveland Rosenblums and they led that team to two straight championships. Nat Holman signed up with the Chicago Bruins owned by George Halas, who also owned the Chicago Bears of the National Football League. Another NFL guy, George Preston Marshall, owner of the Washington Redskins, owned Marshall's Washington Palace Five. That was where George Haggerty landed up.

Although the Celtics were disbursed around the American League, they still had a feel for their old team's habits. In a game between Washington and Chicago, Holman and Haggerty were on opposite sides of the fence. In the closing moments of the game Haggerty of the Palace Five had the ball.

"Hey, George, pass it here," Nat Holman yelled. Haggerty, out of reflex, passed the ball to his longtime teammate, who laid it in and won the game for Chicago. Maybe little things like that put the Celtics back together as a team in 1929.

Celtics home games were played in the 71st Regiment Armory in New York City. Later on they moved into the first and then the second Madison Square Garden. But a lot of the Celtics action was on the road, where they sometimes played more than 150 games a year before large crowds. In 1922 in Cleveland more than 23,000 came out to see them do their thing. The popularity of the Original Celtics made for some big paydays for their players. In the 1920s, their best guys earned $10,000 a year—in that time a great deal of money.

But they earned it. Travel was tough, real tough. The way of life for the Original Celtics was wandering all over the East, the Midwest, the South. There was hardly any rest time, any time to even get their uniforms that they carried from game to game cleaned up, any time for anything much except basketball.

There was no preseason, no trainers, no doctors. Training camp was unheard of. Players got in shape by playing. Pain from injuries was treated with a shot of booze or aspirin or sleep. Guys didn't complain. They played the game. As Joe Lapchick said, "The big asset was guts; the only objective was to win basketball games."

Many of the places the Celtics played on the road were kind of threatening. And to say they lacked the home court advantage in those places is to understate matters.

One of the least favorite places for the Celtics to play was in South Brooklyn, at a dance hall called Prospect Hall. To the Celtics that place was known as the "Bucket of Blood." Not only did they have to contend with the physical play of the opposition in that dance hall, they also had to dodge bottles that were thrown at them by the more excitable fans seated in the rafters above the playing court. Others seated on the sidelines did things far worse. Dutch Dehnert told me that he was used to guys trying to trip him when he was going down the court, but he could never get used to nuts trying to burn him with a lit cigarette when he tried to pass a ball in from out of bounds.

From 1921 to 1928, the Celts won 720 games and lost just 75. One of those seasons they won 204 games against just 11 losses. Those were their real glory years— a time when they won 90% of their games. In the 1930s, the team toured around in a Pierce Arrow car. I don't know if it had a radio, but if it did they could have listened to the *Kate Smith Program* —they were sponsored for a couple of seasons by the lady who sang "God Bless America."

On November 11, 1941, the Celtics became history when they played in Madison Square Garden against a team of players from the New York Football Giants in a preliminary game. It was the last appearance of the Original Celtics.

WOMEN'S BASKETBALL

During the 1920s and 1930s, the popularity of women's
high school and college basketball went downhill. That
was because some educators thought the more sedate
sports were best, and women's basketball wasn't sedate
enough for them.

Outside of the educational system, however, the
slack was picked up by a few business and AAU women's
teams. There were also a couple of good women's pro
basketball teams that began as early as the 1920s. The
best of the lot was the Red Heads, put together in 1936.

They weren't all real redheads—some of those girls
wore wigs or dyed their hair. But that was the only thing
that was phoney about them. They could play basketball,
and they won a very high percentage of their games.

By 1947, with a break in the action because of
World War II, the Red Heads had done their thing before more than two million fans in 46 states. The Red
Heads played using men's rules. Many of their games
were against men's teams. Their style of play was a combination of Harlem Globetrotter flashiness and good,
solid, team basketball.

In those days the Red Heads and other women's
teams took some abuse. Some people called them unfemi-
nine and things worse. So it was kind of tough for women
to make a place for themselves in basketball. Things sure
have changed for the better today—and some of the
change is due to teams like the Red Heads, who were
there first doing their stuff.

Women have made lots of contributions to basketball, and I was pleased to see three of them enshrined in
the Hall of Fame on July 1, 1985. They really had the

credentials. Sendra Berenson-Abbott, called by many the mother of women's basketball, was the first director of physical education at Smith College. In 1892, when she heard the game of basketball had been invented, she contacted Dr. James Naismith and visited him and watched the game being played. The Lithuanian-born educator was the one who came up with the rules for the women's college basketball game, rules that stayed in effect for seventy-five years. She wrote the first women's basketball guide and organized the first basketball committee for women. With all those things that she had going for her, it's no wonder she's in the Hall.

Bertha F. Teague is the winningest high school girl's basketball coach in history with 1,152 victories. Ms. Teague coached at Byng High School in Oklahoma from 1927 to 1969. Her teams piled up amazing stats: 38 conference titles, 27 district championships, and 8 state championships. In all those years, her teams lost just 115 games. They were undefeated in five seasons. In the late '30s, her teams had a string of 98 straight wins. Those stats are outstanding at any level of competition. I spent some time with her in 1985 at the Hall of Fame ceremonies when she was inducted, and I can tell you that she's quite a lady.

The Wade Trophy is presented each year to the top women's collegiate basketball player in the United States. It's named in honor of L. Margaret Wade, who also was enshrined in the Basketball Hall of Fame on July 1, 1985. Ms. Wade retired from coaching in 1979 with a 633-117 career record. She was a star high school and college player and a great high school coach at Cleveland High School in Mississippi. In nineteen years there her teams won 453 and lost just 89 games. Ms. Wade returned to her alma mater, Delta State, in 1973. During her time coaching at Cleveland High, Wade's teams won three consecutive AIAW championships. She was elected to the Mississippi Hall of Fame in 1975. Two years later, the trophy for the best women's collegiate player was named for her. Its first recipient was Carol Blazejowski of Montclair, New Jersey, who received the trophy in March of 1978.

There have been plenty of other outstanding female contributors to basketball who someday, I'm sure, will find their way into the Basketball Hall of Fame. On February 16, 1987, Lynne Lorenzen of Ventura High School in Mason City, Iowa, knocked in 54 points. That gave her a career total of 6,266 points. It was sixteen more points than that of the previous record holder, Denise Long, who was also an Iowa high school player in the '60s. Lorenzen wound up with a total of 6,736 points scored in her high school career.

On January 23, 1981, Annette Kennedy—a small package at 5'5" but a hell of a player for SUNY in Purchase, New York—scored 70 points. That performance gave her team a 116-21—no, that's not a typo—romp over Pratt Institute. That performance also broke the women's collegiate single-game mark of 60 points set in 1978 by Pearl Monroe of Francis Marion College.

The next time someone asks you who the first woman was to ever dunk a basketball in collegiate competition, you can tell them that Red gave you the answer. On December 21, 1984, Georgeann Wells of West Virginia did the dunk.

Marie Boyd is not exactly a household name to basketball fans, but back in the 1920s, what she did was talked about all over the place. On February 25, 1924, playing for Lonaconing Central Maryland, Marie poured in an incredible 156 points to lead her team to a 162-3— again, that's no typo, we're doing our proofreading— over Cumberland Ursuline Academy. Those 156 points that Marie scored still stand as the most ever by a high school girl in a game.

One of the greatest high school girls' basketball teams of all time came out of Baskin, Louisiana. From 1947 through 1953, that team won 218 straight games, the national record for a girls' high school team.

Darlene May is one of the more outstanding contemporary officials in women's basketball. Out of Pomona, California, Ms. May has a couple of firsts to her credit. In August 1977, she became the first woman to officiate a men's international basketball game. It took place at the World University Games in Sofia, Bulgaria—France vs. Italy. Then, on March 23, 1984, Ms. May was picked as the first woman to be an Olympic basketball official. There was women's basketball at the 1976 Montreal and 1980 Moscow Olympics, but the officials at these games were all men. Ms. May did a terrific job officiating at the L.A. Games of the Twenty-Third Olympiad.

Here's another interesting first in women's basketball: Lynette Woodard made her debut with the Harlem Globetrotters in Spokane, Washington, on November 13, 1985. Lynette was the first female Globetrotter.

Still another first took place on September 5, 1979, when Ann Meyers, former Olympic star and four-time all-American at UCLA, became the first woman to sign a contract with an NBA team. Ann signed on the dotted line with the Indiana Pacers, but didn't make the team.

Immaculata College has gotten a few "firsts" and has carved out quite a name for itself in women's basketball. They played in the first women's collegiate game held in Madison Square Garden before a crowd of over 11,000. It took place on February 22, 1975, against Queens College. Exactly a month later, Immaculata was defeated by Delta State, 90-81. That loss was the first in an AIAU tournament game in four years for Immaculata.

I've always thought of Nancy Lieberman as one of the best female players ever. The youngest member of the 1976 Silver Medal U.S. Olympic women's basketball team, Nancy had led Old Dominion to two straight national championships. On March 26, 1980, Nancy received the Margaret Wade Trophy for the second straight year as most outstanding player in women's basketball. In 1981 the flaming redhead, who grew up in my part of the world, Far Rockaway, New York, became the number-one draft choice and superstar of the Dallas Diamonds of the Women's Basketball League.

A couple of years later, Nancy racked up a couple of more firsts. She became the first female team sport player to earn over $1 million. And she was the first woman to play in an organized professional men's basketball league. On June 10, 1986, Nancy played for the Springfield Fame, in the United States Basketball League, against the Staten Island Stallions. They called her "Lady Magic."

"I don't have the respect of the male basketball players that I've competed against because I have red hair and wear high heels," she said. "It's because I can play basketball." She sure can. Every time I've watched her play, I've gotten a big kick out of her.

HIGH SCHOOL BASKETBALL

I can still remember my days playing basketball at Franklin K. Lane High School in Queens. That was another time, another game, but it's still vivid in my mind. A couple of years ago I returned to Lane and they dedicated the gym as the William "Red" Holzman Gymnasium. I got a big kick out of that. But what happened to me has happened over and over again in high school basketball gyms all over the United States—naming a place for a guy or girl who starred on that court. It's one way of showing how important high school basketball is. That's where the road to the NBA and for some the path to the Hall of Fame in Springfield starts.

Just where high school basketball began is a matter that the experts get into debates over. Most of them think that the first teams to play the game were from Holyoke, Massachusetts, and Central High School of Philadelphia. What is known, though, is that some of those early high school teams were so good they played against college teams and whipped the hell out of them.

Probably the most interesting and colorful high school team ever was the 1928 Carr Creek, Kentucky, group. There were only eight kids on that team, all poor country boys. They didn't have any uniforms and they played their home games on an outdoor court. The kindest thing anyone could say about its condition was that it was homemade. The Carr Creek kids got all the way to the state final only to wind up losing in four overtime periods to Ashland High School, 13-11.

What those kids accomplished made them the favorite basketball team in the state of Kentucky. A lot of people raised money and bought the kids uniforms and sent them to the national high school basketball tournament in Chicago. Will Rogers wrote about the team; newspapers all over America gave them coverage.

In Chicago, the Kentucky kids piled up victories over the state champions from New Mexico, Texas, and Connecticut. They were on a roll until they met the state champ from Vienna, Georgia, and went down to defeat. Their accomplishment, however, was cited in Congress, and the kids became the toast of the state of Kentucky. What happened with Carr Creek, Kentucky—eight poor boys getting all that attention and love—is just one of my all-time favorite stories of high school basketball in America.

In New York City in the 1930s Franklin High School and James Madison High both had really outstanding teams that posted all kinds of incredible winning records.

My buddy Fuzzy Levane was on a Madison team with Larry Baxter, Lenny and Howie Rader, Stan Waxman, and Fred Lewis. Incredibly, all of those guys went on to play pro basketball. The Franklin team had Red Phillips and Pop Gates and later Bobby Wanzer. Talk about your great high school teams—I'd bet those two New York City teams could beat any high school team that's ever been.

BLACKS IN BASKETBALL

Everyone knows the story of Jackie Robinson breaking baseball's color line. But the history of blacks and their contribution to the history of basketball has gotten much less play.

Some of you probably know that it wasn't until 1950 that black players were allowed into the NBA. Chuck Cooper of Dusquesne University in Pittsburgh was picked by the Boston Celtics and has the distinction of being the first black drafted into the NBA. That season, Nat "Sweetwater" Clifton left the Harlem Globetrotters to play for the New York Knicks. That made Cooper and Clifton the first blacks in the NBA. But before they arrived on the scene, there was an entire history of black players in professional basketball.

Back in 1946–47, when I was playing for the Rochester Royals, owner-coach Lester Harrison signed Dolly King and Pop Gates. Lester's motto was: "If he can play, he can play." Pop was sold to Buffalo, and Dolly did his thing for my Rochester team.

About 6'5" and very powerfully built, Dolly had been a tremendous baseball, football, and basketball star at Long Island University. I roomed with him and Fuzzy Levane during the '46–47 season. The three of us came from New York City—a Jewish guy, an Italian guy, and a black guy. Fuzzy and I felt sort of protective towards Dolly. We were always aware that he could run into problems. Fortunately, there weren't that many, but there shouldn't have been any. Too bad that a class guy like that had to put up with the few that were. I remember in some of our games on the road, stupid bigots taunted Dolly with racial slurs. We had a mess at the Claypool Hotel in Indianapolis. They refused to serve any food to Dolly in the restaurant. So the whole team wound up eating in the utility room of the kitchen. That was an ugly scene. From that time on, Fuzzy and I joined Dolly on the road eating meals in our hotel room.

A hell of a player, and a hell of a guy, Dolly King hardly ever talked about racial issues. He just went about his business of playing basketball.

The first all-black professional basketball team was the Harlem Renaissance Five, known as the Rens. They came before the Harlem Globetrotters and were a much different kind of team. The Globies clowned around; the Rens played to win and did they win. For their time, there was probably no better basketball team in the world. Along with the Original Celtics and Buffalo Germans, as a team they are enshrined in the Basketball Hall of Fame in Springfield—and rightfully so.

Put together in 1922 by Bob Douglas, the owner of the Renaissance Casino Ballroom in Harlem, the Rens won 473 games and lost just 49 times from 1932 to 1936. That translates to a winning percentage of 91 percent. Between January 1, 1933, and March 27, 1933, the Rens won 88 games in a row. Their streak was stopped by the Celtics. In the Rens' twenty-two years of existence they won 2,318 games and lost just 381.

Most of their games were one-night stands that they traveled to in their own custom-made, specially equipped "$10,000 bus."

On courts they were unfamiliar with, in all kinds of strange places, the Rens played great team basketball. They specialized in a switching, man-to-man defense. It held the opposition's scoring down, and it also saved them steps and energy. In my growing-up years I always liked their style and would watch them in admiration when they came to Arcadia Hall in Brooklyn to play against a team called the Jewels.

Some of the famous players on the Rens included:

Clarence "Fats" Jenkins, Wee Willie Smith, Bill Yancey, James "Pappy" Ricks, John "Casey" Holt, Eyre "Bruiser" Saitch, and Charles "Tarzan" Cooper. Both Yancey and Jenkins were also great stars in Negro League Baseball.

The Rens were so good that in 1926–27 they split a six-game series with the Original Celtics. And in 1933, the Rens took seven of eight games from the Celtics. One of their greatest games in the 1930s took place on February 16, 1935. Playing against the Celtics in Kansas City, the Rens displayed superb ball control for the last six minutes and held on to win the game by one point.

Maybe it was the success of the Rens that gave Abe Saperstein the idea to start the Harlem Globetrotters in January of 1927. As the story goes, though, it was something else. Abe had founded the team in 1926 to play in Chicago's Savoy Ballroom. However, the dance hall failed to do much business and was turned into a skating rink. Abe's team didn't know how to skate so they were left without a place to play. It was then that he took five guys, a broken down flivver (that's a car for those of you who don't know the word), and a worn road map and began one of basketball's great attractions.

None of the players were from New York City, much less Harlem, but Abe dreamed up the name Harlem Globetrotters for them anyway. "I used 'Harlem,'" he explained, "because I wanted people to know the team was Negro and 'Globetrotters' because I wanted people to know we'd get around."

They did get around. Through rain storms and blizzards, the Globies did their thing in those early years in places like Juneau, Alaska; Roseberg, Oregon; and Yakima, Washington. Sometimes the Globetrotters made their way by dogsled or by horse and wagon, but they got to where they were going. They played any team in any place. At the start there was no clowning and they usually beat the hell out of the competition. After a while no one wanted to play them, so they added all of those funny and special touches that have become the trademark of the team—and started winning by smaller margins. That almost guaranteed a happy crowd and a return engagement.

More than sixty-five years later, that seems to have worked: our "Ambassadors of Good Will" have played before millions in more than a hundred countries.

Among those who have played for the Globetrotters are Bob Gibson, the former great pitching star for the St. Louis Cardinals, Wilt Chamberlain, "Sweetwater" Clifton, Connie Hawkins, Ermer Robinson, a guy from San Diego whose specialty was the one-hand push shot, and Clarence Wilson, from Horse Cave, Kentucky, who could shoot the set shot with the best of them.

The two greatest attractions the Globetrotters ever had were Reece "Goose" Tatum and Marcus Haynes. Tatum was called "The Clown Prince of Basketball" and had an arm span of eighty-four inches—those arms went all the way down to his knees. Haynes could dribble— behind his back, between his legs, or through the legs of an opposing player.

In the summer of 1954 I was near the end of my playing career. I didn't quite realize how near. To earn a little extra cash I hooked up for two weeks with a touring team that played against the Globetrotters. Our basketball games were played in major league baseball parks while the home team was on the road. It was quite an experience for me being around those guys, and I like to think it was an experience for them.

I'll never forget watching Goose Tatum night after night. The man was a born showman, a great entertainer. He had all those loose moves, that great athletic ability, and a great sense of humor. One of his special weapons was a terrific hook shot that he threw up with a kind of wild abandon at any time in the game and it seemed from almost any place on the court. And he usually scored with it. Wearing an old slouch hat, faking guys left, right, sideways—Goose was funnier than any clown.

Goose was the star of stars of the Harlem Globetrotters. Appropriately, his transportation was a big white Cadillac. We played those games through the summertime heat, and the other guys on the Globies were always anxious to get into the cool air conditioning of Goose's Cadillac. He never objected; there was just one condition that he laid down. All the guys had to sit in the front of the Caddy and one of them had to drive. Nobody sat in the back of that big car except for the Goose.

A few days of the tour had passed when I noticed that the Globetrotters were having arguments before games. In those arguments my name always came up. I eavesdropped.

"Tonight's my night for guarding Holzman."

"You had him last night."

"I know, but I can still use some rest."

"I'll give you a few bucks—let me have him."

"You can have him, but it'll cost you more than a few bucks. Getting a rest guarding that old Holzman is worth more than a few bucks."

In past years, there had usually been discussions about how to guard me. Now the spirited debate over who was to guard me and when did a lot to dash any thought I might have harbored of playing on for another year in the NBA. What the Globetrotters had to say about me wasn't the deciding factor, but it was one of the reasons that I went out as an active player and decided to concentrate all my remaining energies on coaching. And with some of those teams I coached I needed all my remaining energies.

2

The Five-Ring Circus

eople nowadays watch basketball in the Olympics never realizing the hard time the sport had getting to be an official Olympic sport. Back in 1928, Forrest (Phog) Allen was pushing to get the game into the Olympics in Amsterdam as an international demonstration sport. It was no dice. It was lacrosse that was picked instead. Then in 1932 at the L.A. Games, Allen and his supporters pushed again to get basketball into the Olympics. And again it was turned down in favor of lacrosse. Some people back then had a thing with lacrosse.

Finally, in 1936 in Berlin, basketball made its debut as an official Olympic sport. I was sixteen years old then and doing pretty good on the basketball court at Franklin K. Lane High School in Brooklyn, and I had a passing thought of what it might be like to try out for the Olympic team—but it was only a passing thought.

Phog Allen came up with the idea of sending James Naismith over to Berlin to have the thrill of seeing the game he invented played in the Olympics. Naismith got to Berlin, but there was a bit of a screwup. He arrived without a pass to any of the basketball games. When he finally was given a pass for all the games, his name was ignored and he was dropped off the pass list. Things got better for the good doctor, though. After everyone realized who he was he got the honor of throwing out the ball for the first game between France and Estonia. And he was shown a lot of honor in a special ceremony at the Hall of German Sports.

There was some controversy back then—it seems there's always controversy in the Olympics. The International Basketball Federation ruled that guys 6'3" and over couldn't play. Three of the USA players were that tall or taller, and they would have been off the team if that rule stood. The U.S. protested, and the rule against the big guys was dropped.

They should have also done something about the playing conditions. Games were outdoors in a tennis stadium. That always reminded me of my days coaching outdoors in Puerto Rico. On the day of the Olympic final the whole place was flooded by a lot of rain. The playing surface, dirt to begin with, became pure mud. And dribbling on that stuff was mushy going. So, to avoid the mushy going, there was no dribbling. There were also no fans in the stands—those few who were there watched that championship game from inside their parked cars. The U.S. team won the gold medal, beating Canada 19-8. That's not a typo—that was the final score. That mud was tough. Joe Fortenberry, a 6'8" center from McPherson, Kansas, knocked in eight points—one more and he would have outscored the whole Canadian team.

The U.S. team was a collection of thirteen AAU players and one guy from the University of Washington. Seven guys came from the Universal Pictures Corporation team out of Hollywood and they brought their coach along with them—James Needles. Somebody said they were a bunch of role players. Six other guys came from the Globe Oil and Refining Company of McPherson, Kansas.

That Olympics is remembered as the "Nazi Olympics" and Sam Balter, a member of our Olympic basketball team and the first Jewish athlete chosen for the Games, remembered the time well.

"I was very conscious of being Jewish and going to the Games," said Balter, who went on to become a popular sports columnist and broadcaster on the West Coast. "When we arrived we were driven through the streets in open-air buses and were greeted by several million Germans. Then we stopped at City Hall, where Goering was to speak. The first sound I remember hearing was a rat-a-tat-tat. I thought it was a machine gun. It turned out that it was only the band striking up."

World War II cancelled the Olympics in 1940 and '44. London was the site of the 1948 Games, and the U.S. basketball team was picked as it had been in the past through a tournament competition. Kentucky, the NCAA champion, and the Phillips 66ers or Oilers, the AAU champ, met in the final game in New York City.

Phillips had been the top-rated company team for years. Bob Kurland, a seven-footer from Oklahoma A&M, had chosen not to turn pro. Instead he plied his trade as the star of the Phillips team and enjoyed a good career in business in Bartlesville, Oklahoma, home of the 66ers. I ran into Bob recently and he's still working for the 66ers. The Kentucky team had Alex Groza, Cliff Barker, Ralph Beard, Wah Wah Jones, and Kenny Rollins, and was coached by the Baron—Adolph Rupp.

The two teams met in Madison Square Garden. Behind Kurland's twenty points and his outplaying of Groza, who he held to one field goal and two free throws, the 66ers beat Kentucky by four points. All five Kentucky starters were chosen for the Olympic team as well as all five Phillips starters. The only hitch in that was that as losing coach Rupp was made the assistant basketball coach for the Olympic team. Omar (Bud) Browning of Phillips was given the head coach slot. That kind of teed Rupp off but he had to live with it.

That '48 Olympics had all kinds of odd moments and interesting things going on. Kurland, the U.S. center, had a lot of his height in his legs. It proved to be a good thing for a Chinese player who dribbled the ball right through Bob's legs and wound up scoring a basket.

I don't know what got the spectators more excited— the sight of a player losing his pants, or a ref getting kayoed, but both of those things took place on the basketball court during those '48 games. The ref, who was British, got his during a prelim game between Iraq and Chile. The guy who lost his shorts was a Brazilian, and he got sent off the court and back to the dressing room to cover up.

The worst team in the whole tournament was Iraq. Twice it lost by 100 points—giving up points proved to be its speciality. The opposition averaged 104 points a game against Iraq, who averaged just 23.5 a game on offense.

Many of the guys who have played Olympic basketball have gone on to fame and fortune. Llanusa Gobel, a member of the Cuban team, went on to become Fidel Castro's Minister of Education.

The U.S. team was so loaded with talent that it won all eight of its games, scoring 524 points to the opposition's 256. Cliff Barker, Alex Groza, Ralph Beard, Don Barksdale, Wah Wah Jones—all the stars from the University of Kentucky basketball team went on to become members of the Indianapolis Olympians in the NBA. Vince Boryla and Ray Lumpp also made it big in the pros after playing for our '48 Olympic basketball team. Alex Groza and Bob Kurland were the big gunners—Groza scored 76 points in the eight games he played, while Kurland kicked in with 65 points.

The 1952 Olympics were staged in Helsinki, Finland. Bob Kurland was back for his second time as a member of our basketball team, but the big star was Clyde Lovellette of Kansas, who would have a fine NBA career and wind up as a member of the Basketball Hall of Fame.

That competition showcased the rivalry between the U.S. and Russia. We destroyed the Soviets in a semifinal game 86-58. The championship game was a rematch. The Russians played slow-down basketball. After the first ten minutes of the game we led 4-2. Again—that's not a typo. Only six points were scored in the first ten minutes because of the Russian stalling tactics. Things then sped up a little—but only a little. At the half the score was 17-15. Lovellette scored with five minutes to play in the game, giving our team a 31-25

lead, and then we slowed things down. One of the Russian players was so mad he took a seat on the floor and
watched the slo-mo action. But then his coach got on his
case, ordering him to get up.

The final score was U.S. 36, U.S.S.R. 25.

I've heard about some rough moments out on the
basketball court and seen some of them take place. But
the action in the '52 Olympics was in a class by itself.
Most of it was caused by the team from Uruguay. In a
semifinal game, players from that team and some of their
supporters beat the stuffing out of an American ref. Two
of the Uruguayan players were banned from the rest of
the competition. A couple of days later Uruguay played
Russia, and the match was so physical that three of
the Russian players had to get first aid treatment. In
the match for third place between Uruguay and Argentina, another big fight took place with a couple of
dozen people involved. When the dust cleared and all the
fouls had been called, Uruguay had only four players left
and Argentina had only three remaining to finish the
game. That wasn't basketball; it was a boxing match.

The 1956 Games were more peaceful. The U.S.
team coasted to eight straight wins and the gold medal.
There weren't too many household names on the
U.S. team except for Bill Russell and K.C. Jones. That
was enough. Russell and Jones were teammates at San
Francisco University, on the Olympic team, and then on
the Boston Celtics. They knew how to win. Four times
that '52 team scored over 100 points—their average
margin of victory in each game was 30 points or more.

In 1960, the greatest Olympic basketball team of
all time was put together. It was a coach's dream team.
They could have beaten almost anybody, including
many of the NBA teams. That team, which went 8-0 in

Rome and outscored the opposition 815-476, included Jerry West, Oscar Robertson, Jerry Lucas, Walt Bellamy, Darrall Imhoff, Terry Dischinger, Bob Boozer, and John Havlicek, who was able to qualify only as an alternate. Ten players from that Olympic team that averaged over 102 points a game made the NBA. Four players off that team made the basketball Hall of Fame. And all four of those guys also are on my list of franchise players.

In 1964 in Tokyo our team went 9-0 and beat Russia in the gold medal game, 73-59. That U.S. team wasn't as strong as the '60 club, but it had some top players to go along with Bill Bradley: Jim "Bad News" Barnes, Mel Counts, Walt Hazzard, Lucious Jackson, and Jeff Mullins. The squad from Peru finished way out of the pack, but it got lots of attention from the media because four Duarte brothers were on that team: Ricardo, Raul, Luis, and Enrique.

There were even more politics than usual for the '68 Games in Mexico City. A threatened black power boycott affected things and cut down on some of the talent on our basketball team. Kareem Abdul-Jabbar said he didn't want to take time off from his studies and also said he sympathized with the black power boycott and didn't show. Others went along with him. Elvin Hayes wasn't there either, but that was because he had already signed a pro contract. The U.S. team still had talent: JoJo White, Spencer Haywood, Charlie Scott, Bill Hosket, and others. It was enough talent for the team to go 9-0 and win the gold, beating Yugoslavia 65-50 in the final game as Spencer Haywood and JoJo White turned things up a notch.

Starting in 1936 when the U.S. basketball team defeated Estonia 52-28, we had never lost an Olympic basketball game. Going into the final match in the 1972 Olympics in Munich against the Soviets the U.S. winning streak was sixty-three games, including three final match wins over the Russians.

Doug Collins, Bobby Jones, and Tom McMillen were a few of the guys on that '72 team who made the NBA. Each of them has had many big moments, but they'll never forget what happened in the Olympics.

With three seconds left to play in the game, the Russians, to everyone's surprise, had a 49-48 lead. Then a Russian player must have had a mental lapse. He threw the ball to Doug Collins, who was intentionally fouled by two charging Russian players and was knocked unconscious. When he came to, he sank two foul shots. The U.S. team started to celebrate, thinking time had run out and they had won the game. But one of the officials said there was still a second left in the game. The Russians threw the ball the length of the court but couldn't manage to score. Time ran out. Then the head official, who technically had no right to even get into the act, added three more seconds to the clock. It was like instant-replay time, and also like a three-ring circus out there. It also seemed as if the Russians were going to be given a chance to shoot until they scored and won the game.

That's exactly what happened. A jam by the Soviet center, Alexsandr Belov, gave the U.S.S.R. a 51-50 win and gave the U.S. its first loss ever in Olympic basketball.

A protest was filed by the U.S. Olympic Committee. Then Hank Iba, the U.S. basketball coach, got his pocket picked both literally and figuratively. Unbelievably, when he signed the official protest his pocket was picked. Hank not only lost his wallet and the 370 bucks in it but the U.S. also lost out on its protest. Our guys were so mad that they refused to accept the second place silver medal.

The 1976 Summer Olympics took place in Montreal. In the four years that had passed since our team "lost" to the Russians, there was a lot of anticipation of the rematch. The '76 U.S. team had guys like Phil Ford, Adrian Dantley (the high scorer in the tournament with over 19 points a game), Walter Davis, Quinn Buckner, Ernie Grunfeld, Scott May and Mitch Kupchak. It was a good, solid team.

The rematch never came off. Yugoslavia upset the Russians, 89-84. And the U.S. team was also almost upset by Puerto Rico in the second game of the tournament. The team from Puerto Rico was led by Butch Lee of Marquette University. Playing for his native country, Lee scored 35 points, hitting 15 of 18 shots from the field. If he had hit one more, Puerto Rico would have won. As it was they lost by a point to the U.S. team.

The championship game for the gold medal saw the U.S. rack up Yugoslavia, 95-74. That was a big win and gave our guys a 7-0 record in the tournament. But the other countries were getting better and the competition was getting closer. The U.S. team scored 584 points and gave up 500. That stat showed how basketball skills were spreading worldwide.

Yugoslavia won the gold medal in 1980 in the Games in Moscow that were boycotted by the U.S. and many other countries. The Russians finished in third place. India was the whipping boy for all the teams, losing all of its games by big margins.

In the L.A. Games in 1984 it was no contest on the basketball court. The U.S. team, coached by Bobby Knight, featured Michael Jordan, Patrick Ewing,

Wayman Tisdale, Leon Wood, Alvin Robertson, Chris Mullin, Sam Perkins, Steve Alford, and Vern Fleming— a group of guys whose best years are still ahead of them in the NBA.

The U.S. team went 8-0, won the gold, and outscored the opposition 763-506. Our guys won each game by an average of 32 points. Jordan averaged over seven a game; Ewing led all of the players in the tournament in blocked shots while Leon Wood was the top assists guy. We had a powerful and balanced team and it showed. The gold medal game with Spain was a laugher. The U.S. won 96-65.

There were a lot of interesting quotes that came out after all the action was over. Some said that the U.S. victory was a little tarnished because Russia had boycotted the Games.

"I want to dispel one thing," Bobby Knight said. "We could beat the Soviet Union any time they want to play us."

The coach of Spain whose team lost in the final game said, "The United States of America is at least fifty years ahead of the rest of the basketball world."

With that gold medal in the books the U.S. had a record of 77-1 in the Olympic Games. No other nation has ever dominated a single sport the way we have.

The U.S. women defeated Korea 85-55 in the championship game in '84 to give America its first gold medal in Olympic basketball for women. That made it a gold and a silver for the U.S. in two tries. We got the silver in 1976 as Nancy Lieberman did her thing.

In the 1988 Olympics at Seoul, it seemed to everyone that the U.S. men's basketball team was a shoo-in to win the gold medal. It was a star-studded team that had guys like Danny Manning, David Robinson, Mitch

Richmond, and Hersey Hawkins, and it was coached by John Thompson of Georgetown.

But things didn't work out the way the script called for.

The Soviets trimmed the U.S. in the semi-final game 76-63. Part of the reason for the upset was the shooting of Rimas Kourtinaitis, a three-point specialist. The guy hit four out of ten from long range and wound up with 28 points in the game.

"He's not very strong," said Soviet Coach Alexander Gomelski, "but we had special plays for this guy. He gets into good three-point position."

Thompson was put in the position of defending the choices of players he had picked for the U.S. squad, of defending the defensive style of play he made his team use, and of defending how he shuttled players in and out of the game.

"We played extremely hard," Thompson said. "We are extremely disappointed, but there will be life after. They gave their all to represent their country. That is all that can be asked of them . . . I think they will let us back into the country."

Thompson was also a bit annoyed at the fact that NBA teams had played against the Soviets during the summer of '88, something that he thought especially helped the Soviet 7'3" center Arvydas Sabonis.

"He worked hard all summer," Thompson said. "What do you think, he's not going to improve playing against America's finest?"

In fairness to John Thompson, that game against the Soviets showed just how much progress the rest of the world has made in international basketball competition. The loss for the U.S. was only its second in 87 Olympic contests.

A 78-49 bronze medal victory for the Americans over Australia was no consolation prize for the U.S. guys. "That loss to the Russians," Danny Manning said, "is one of the biggest disappointments of my life. It's hard to take any way you look at it."

On the other side of the coin, the American women did what the American men couldn't do. They beat the Soviets 102-88 in the semifinals. Although the Russian women had a big height advantage, the Americans were too fast and too team-oriented to let that stop them. They just ran past the Russian women. Cynthia Cooper put in 27 points and chipped in with this comment: "Now we have proven for certain that we are the best in the world. We knew it. Now the Russians know it, too."

The gold medal game against Yugoslavia was kind of anti-climactic as the U.S. women won 77-70. An inspirational part of the U.S. win was the story of their coach, Kay Yow. A short time after she was picked to head up the team she learned that she had breast cancer. Yow underwent a modified radical mastectomy and completely recovered.

"I like to have a mission," she said. "Beating cancer was a mission. Now winning the gold is another mission. A year ago I never thought I'd be a part of it. I can't tell you what it means to have seen this day."

These same feelings were echoed by Theresa Edwards, Cynthia Cooper, Suzie McConnell, Anne Donovan, Bridgette Gordon, and the other women on that exciting 1988 U.S. women's Olympic basketball team that got the gold and made up a little bit for the disappointment felt by the men's team.

The 1988 Olympics raised a lot of people's consciousness about the kind of talent that is playing basketball in countries all over the world. Everyone knows that now Eastern European players are playing in the NBA—Drazen Petrovic (New Jersey Nets), Milos Babic (Cleveland Cavaliers), Vlade Divac (Los Angeles Lakers), and Stojan Vrankovic (Boston Celtics) are all from Yugoslavia, while Sarunas Marciulionis (Golden State Warriors) hails from Lithuania and Aleksandr Volkov (Atlanta Hawks) from Russia. But guys with foreign roots on NBA rosters is not something new. There are quite a few guys now in action whose birthplace was outside of the United States.

Patrick Ewing of the Knicks was born in Jamaica while Detlef Schrempf of Indiana came from West Germany. Another big guy for the Pacers, Rik Smits, is from the Netherlands. On the Dallas Mavericks, James Donaldson was born in England while Rolando Blackman was born in Panama.

Africa claims two of the big men in the NBA. Manute Bol, all 7'5" of him, comes from the Sudan, and Houston's Hakeem Olajuwon hails from Nigeria. The only player from France is Jacques Dominique Wilkins, who plays for the Atlanta Hawks.

Other guys with foreign birthplaces include: Mychal Thompson of the Los Angeles Lakers—the Bahamas; Bill Wennington of Sacramento—Canada; Kiki Vanderweghe of New York—Germany; Mike Smrek of the Los Angeles Clippers—Canada; Olden Polynice of the Clippers—Haiti; Alaa Abdelnaby of the Portland Trail Blazers—Egypt; and Rony Seikaly of the Miami Heat—Lebanon.

Speaking of guys who were born in other countries and came over to play in the NBA, during the 1985–1986 season the Phoenix Suns had a rookie forward named Georgi Glouchkov from Bulgaria. When he reported to training camp, they said he knew two English phrases: "Phoenix Suns" and "pretty girl." It didn't take the Bulgarian long to learn a few more phrases like "large O.J.," "give me five," and "vodka, no ice."

3

Odds and Ends:

from Ossie Schectman to Bevo Francis

or all of you up on trivia, oddities, and unusual hoop happenings, this section of the book is for you.

There was a big fuss and a lot of publicity on January 25, 1988, when Rickey Green of the Utah Jazz scored the 5-millionth point in NBA history. I was around when the first two points were scored in the first year of the NBA's existence. Ossie Schectman of the Knicks took a bounce pass from Leo Gottlieb and hit a driving layup to give the Knicks a 2-0 start against the Toronto Huskies. Schectman scored eleven points in that game as the Knicks defeated Toronto, 68-66.

The way the basketball goes round and round was really brought home to me at the start of the NBA 1988–89 season. At Miami's first game in the NBA ever, there was Ossie

Schectman throwing out the first ball. And there was Miami coach Ron Rothstein, whose father was my teammate way back when I played basketball at Local 102. I guess that also makes me the first trucker ever to be admitted to the Hall of Fame.

Schectman, Rothstein, and so many others are part of the growing list of NBA firsts. Some of those "firsts" are really one for the book—this book.

One of my favorites took place on March 23, 1979. New Jersey and Philadelphia went at it, replaying the final 17 minutes and 50 seconds of a game that was originally played on November 8, 1978. The original game was protested when a third technical foul was called on Nets Coach Kevin Loughery and Bernard King. The protest was upheld because under NBA rules, three technical fouls is overkill. Only two T's can be called in a game on any player or coach.

The game was replayed from the point of protest. Philly was leading 84-81 with 5:50 remaining in the third quarter. The 76ers eventually wound up winning the game, 123-117.

What made that replayed game especially unusual was that in the time that passed between the original game and the continuation, four players changed teams. Harvey Catchings and Ralph Simpson moved from Philadelphia to New Jersey, while Eric Money and Al Skinner went from the Nets to the Sixers. All four guys were listed in the lineups for both teams in the final boxscores. Nothing like that ever happened before in the NBA's thirty-four years.

During my playing days I was personally a part of a few oddities that happened once—once was enough—in the league.

On January 6, 1951, a very cold night in Rochester, my Royals played against the Indianapolis Olympians in the longest game in NBA history.

Every time I think about that game I wince. It was dull and boring basketball. It lasted and lasted through six overtime periods. Some of our hometown fans booed and hundreds of others walked out of the old Edgerton Park Arena—they couldn't take the slow-down, stalling tactics.

It lasted a grand total of 78 minutes including the six overtimes. In those overtimes a total of just 23 shots were taken. Players just stood around staring at each other while one guy dribbled, looking to make a smart pass for a high percentage shot. Back then I was in great shape, but my butt was dragging when that marathon mercifully came to an end. We wound up losing the game to Indianapolis, 75-73. I played all but 2 of those 78 minutes, probably an NBA record and a first, but I never received credit. That's because stats for minutes played in a game did not become official until the following season.

Near the end of my playing career I was involved in another "first." I was a member of the Milwaukee Hawks and we were scheduled to play Baltimore at home on the last day of the season and then go to Baltimore for the final game for both teams. Both teams were out of the race, long out of the race, so the games meant nothing to either of us. Ben Kerner, the Milwaukee owner, was eager to save a little money and was able to convince Baltimore's management to play both games as a doubleheader in Milwaukee. We played. We beat Baltimore in both games. And I was the star in each game. That's the first time that ever happened. No, not me being the star . . . the same two teams playing each other in an NBA doubleheader.

Another "first" and "last" took place on April 20, 1971. On that date Dave Cowens of Boston and Geoff Petrie of Buffalo became the only co-winners of the Rookie of the Year award in NBA history. Cowens averaged 17 points a game that season and 15 rebounds. Petrie became only the seventh rookie to that point in time to score more than 2,000 points in a season, averaging 24.8 points a game.

The only gorilla that was ever an NBA mascot is also a "first" and "last" and part of history now. For eight seasons Henry Rojas dressed up in his gorilla suit and entertained the fans of the Phoenix Suns. He was even picked to be the official mascot for the 1984 NBA All Star Game.

The big gorilla "retired" after the 1987–88 season, and one thing you can say about him—he went out in style. The Suns presented him with a ton of bananas. Former Phoenix coach John MacLeod sent along one of his favorite neckties as a farewell gift, and Al Bianchi, once a Phoenix assistant coach, gave a retired clipboard to the cause. The guy who was probably the most generous was entertainer Michael Jackson. He sent a telegram, an autographed picture, and a special recording of his latest hit. All of those things were Jackson's way of thanking the gorilla for his patented Michael Jackson moonwalk impersonation.

Tony Lavelli was a guy who did a pretty good impersonation of someone playing the accordion, but that was not a true first. Back on December 22, 1949, in his thirteenth game as a Celtic, Lavelli scored 26 points as Boston defeated Minneapolis. At halftime, Lavelli did double duty by playing the accordion in a mini-concert for the 5,206 fans at Boston Garden. That performance was one of about two dozen that Lavelli gave around the league. The NBA paid him the grand sum of $125 per gig, and Lavelli didn't even have to change uniforms.

Talk about changing uniforms—another interesting first took place in 1949–50. That year a group of guys got together to form an NBA franchise. They could have done what they did without changing uniforms. They were known as the Indianapolis Olympians, and the bulk of talent on that team was the stars of the Kentucky University club that competed in the 1948 Olympics. Cliff Barker, a rookie in the league, coached the Olympians. Ralph Beard, a super guard, was vice-president. The secretary was another player, "Wah Wah" Jones, while still another, Joe Holland, was team treasurer. The club president was "Babe" Kimbrough, out of Lexington, Kentucky, who had graduated with the team. The big star on the Olympians was Alex Groza. That season the 6'7" forward averaged 23.4 points a game, second only to George Mikan. With all that talent Indianapolis finished first in the Western Division.

Some people think it's a bit unusual that Pat Riley was once a broadcaster for the Lakers and then left the booth to become L.A. coach. But an even more unusual job switch took place in the 1950s.

Charlie Eckman traded in his NBA ref's uniform for the plain clothes of an NBA coach without missing a call. And that *was* a first. Back in those days many NBA owners didn't think coaches were that important. Fred Zollner, owner of the Ft. Wayne Pistons, was one of the prime examples of guys with that philosophy.

Eckman and Zollner got to be kind of friendly when the Piston owner used to give Charlie lifts in his private plane for home-and-home series. It was on those plane

rides that Zollner realized firsthand just how much Eck-
man knew about basketball. One thing was for certain—
Charlie knew the rule book backwards and forwards. So
Zollner hired Charlie as his coach.

He was the perfect coach for that team. It was a
ready-made ball club of stars like Max Zaslofky, Larry
Foust, and Mel Hutchins. Eckman would smoke a cigar
and brag, "I'm not a coach. I'm just a cheerleader. I just
throw the ball out there and let them do their stuff.
There's only two good plays in basketball anyway—*South
Pacific* and putting the ball in the hoop."

Charlie coached the Pistons in the 1954–55 season
to a 43-29 record. The next year the Pistons were 37-35.
But Charlie was still riding high—he coached the All
Star team both of those seasons. Then the bottom fell
out. He got Ft. Wayne off to a 9-16 start and was replaced by Ichabod Crane look-alike Red Rocha, a guy
who is my pick for the all-time average NBA player. That
didn't faze Charlie Eckman one bit. What he had done
was an NBA first; and it earned him a place in *Holzman
on Hoops*.

Another one and only moment in pro basketball
history took place in 1948–49. Al Cervi became the
first and only guy to win the Coach of the Year and also
the Most Valuable Player award in the same season.

Cervi was probably the first great pro player who
never went to college, which was even then the tradi-
tional route to the pros. We all called him "The Digger"
because of the way he played. Al was always a bit sensitive
that he had not gone to college and that drove him even
more. Whenever he was matched up against a guy who
had been a college all-American Al would go out of his
way to outdo the guy.

Ironically, I never even saw Al Cervi play when he was in his prime. I was twenty-six years old when Cervi joined my Rochester Royals team in 1945–46. And although he was three or four years older than me, he was a dynamo. I always wondered what he must have been like when he was twenty-one or so. The people in Springfield gave Al his due a couple of years ago when they admitted him to the Basketball Hall of Fame.

Today everyone makes a fuss about Spud Webb, but back in basketball's ancient history there was a guy even smaller than Spud. At five foot three, Barney Sedran was one of the smallest pro players of all time and also one of the greatest players of his era. Little Barney played from 1911–23 for such teams as the Cleveland Rosenblums, the New York Whirlwinds, and the Philadelphia Jaspers. He teamed with a guy named Max "Marty" Friedman who was just a mite bigger than him at 5′8″. Fans called them the "Busy Izzies." After his playing career was over Barney coached all over the place for such teams as the Brooklyn Jewels, the Kate Smith Celtics, and the New England Bombers. I came into contact with him in Troy, New York. He was my coach at Troy when I was freelancing before I broke into the National Basketball League.

The lowest-scoring game and the highest-scoring game in NBA history took place almost exactly thirty-three years apart. On November 22, 1950, at Minneapolis, the Ft. Wayne Pistons defeated the Lakers 19-18. Big George Mikan of the Lakers scored 15 points—10 more than any other player on either team. The game was an exercise in slow motion—especially for the 7,021 fans in attendance. The fourth quarter of that game was *super* slow-mo—Ft. Wayne scored three points and Minnesota scored one. That lowest-scoring game in NBA history and others like it made it clear to everyone that a shot clock was needed, and was one of the big reasons why the 24-second shot clock came into existence.

The highest-scoring game took place on December 13, 1983, at Denver. It took three overtime periods and three hours and eleven minutes before the Detroit Pistons managed their 186-184 win over the Nuggets. Isiah Thomas of the Pistons and Alex English of the Nuggets each scored 47 points. John Long of Detroit knocked in 41 more. But the high scorer for both teams was Kiki Vandeweghe with 51 points. Vandeweghe and English both played fifty minutes and Isiah played fifty-two minutes. I know their tails were dragging and their arms were probably weary from putting up all those hoops.

The attendance in the NBA keeps getting bigger and bigger each year. But teams will have to go a long way before they break the all-time regular-season record of 61,983. That was set on January 29, 1988, at the Silverdome in Detroit when the Boston Celtics played the Pistons. The all-time attendance record for one game of hoops was set back in 1951. A crowd of 75,000 showed up at Berlin's Olympic Stadium to watch the Harlem Globetrotters do their thing. The second-biggest crowd ever to watch a collegiate basketball game was at the NCAA championship in the New Orleans Superdome on March 27 and then again on March 29, 1982. A crowd of 61,612 showed up on both dates. But the biggest crowd to watch a college basketball game was 64,949 on March 24, 1987, at an NCAA Division I semi-final.

The largest crowd ever to see a basketball game in the United States was on hand on July 9, 1984, at the Indianapolis Hoosier Dome. The U.S. Olympic Men's Team beat an NBA All-Star squad 97-82. For openers, the U.S. Women's Olympic Team defeated a collegiate All-Star squad 97-54. And there were 67,596 watching all the action.

The '86–87 season in the NBA had a lot of highlights. For Kareem Abdul-Jabbar and Hakeem Olajuwon it was a time of individual milestones. Those big guys hit the first three-point shots of their careers. It took Kareem eighteen seasons to do it. Akeem knocked in his first three pointer in his third pro season.

Lots of guys have been on NCAA championship teams and NBA championship teams. Only four players ever did the trick in back-to-back years: Bill Russell with San Francisco and the Celtics; Henry Bibby, who I coached, with UCLA and the Knicks; Magic Johnson with Michigan and the Lakers; and Billy Thompson with Louisville and then L.A.

The next time someone asks you what Jack Twyman, Sandy Koufax, and tennis great Tony Trabert have in common, you'll be able to give that guy the correct answer. All three were members of the 1953–54 University of Cincinnati basketball team. Sandy was on the freshman team. Trabert was a sub for half a season. And Jack was the big gun and big star.

Back on February 21, 1952, there was a game played and given the catchy name "Milkman's Special." It's a good thing they don't do things like that in the NBA any more. What happened was the Celtics played the Fort Wayne Pistons at Boston Gardens in a game that tipped off at midnight. The Celts-Piston game came after the Ice Follies had cooled off the parquet floor. There were only 2,368 fans on hand—who knows how many were awake—to see Bob Cousy score 24 points and lead Boston to an 88-67 win in the wee small hours of the morning.

Another interesting special event-type game took place at Madison Square Garden in a pre-game ceremony. The occasion was Julius Erving's last trip to the Garden. The date was April 6, 1987. On hand to bid the "Doctor" farewell were a lot of other doctors: Dr. Ruth Westheimer, Dr. Kildare (Richard Chamberlain), Dr. Joyce Brothers, Dr. K (Dwight Gooden), Dr. McCoy of *Star Trek* (DeForest Kelley), Dr. Seuss, the famous children's author, Dr. Frank Field, the meteorologist, Dr. Steven Hardey of *General Hospital* (Johnny Berardino), Marcus Welby, M.D. (Robert Young), Dr. Henry Kissinger, and Dr. Clifford Huxtable (Bill Cosby). My co-author, Dr. Harvey Frommer, was also there. There was definitely a doctor in the house that night.

Lots of guys have gotten egg on their faces playing pro basketball. There are air balls thrown, passes thrown to the opposition, six guys on the court . . . There have even been instances where guys have lost their shorts. But Paul Mokeski, playing for Milwaukee on May 7, 1986, notched a negative record that probably nobody will ever break. The big guy fouled out after playing just six minutes in the Bucks' 113-108 win over Philadelphia. It was the swiftest disqualification of a player in playoff history.

Speaking of negative records, Danny Ainge of the Boston Celtics has had a pretty positive NBA career. But the *NBA Register* credits him with some sub-par stats compiled during Danny's four-year professional baseball career. The only player to have non-basketball stats included in his profile in the official *NBA Register*, Danny's numbers reveal that in 211 games as a major leaguer, he batted just .220 and managed only two home runs.

On the subject of embarrassing figures, a classic case took place on November 14, 1946. The Boston Celtics lost a game to the St. Louis Bombers when Celt substitute Al Brightman reported to the St. Louis radio announcer instead of to the official scorer. Brightman's embarrassing moment came with Boston ahead in the game by a point with less than one minute remaining. The Celtics were hit with a technical foul—players, Brightman should have known, have to check in with the official scorer, not the radio announcer. Brightman's boo-boo caused the Celtics to lose the game by one point.

Here's an NBA oddity that's always amused me. On January 5, 1986, Phoenix vs. Seattle with 10:48 left in the second quarter and the Suns losing 35-24, the game was stopped. The roof was leaking in the Seattle Coliseum, and the game was called because of rain. You've got to remember that I'm a guy who once coached in Puerto Rico. When the monsoons came, they would get some kids to mop things up. I guess they didn't have any mops around in Seattle that day.

When you talk about winning streaks, here's one that's definitely good enough for this book. On January 14, 1987, Giles Elementary School of Norridge, Illinois, lost to John Mills School 24-22 at Elmwood Park, Illinois. That loss broke the five-year, 221-game winning streak of the Giles Elementary School cagers.

On November 17, 1984, Kansas Newman College performed a trick that reminded me of the way we used to travel in the old days. The Wichita team knocked off Baker University 91-68 on its home court in an afternoon game. That night, they made it two wins in eight hours as they travelled to Hillsboro, Kansas, and knocked off Tabor College 90-79.

Red Auerbach has made a lot of basketball history. On January 10, 1967, Red was brought out of his recent retirement to coach the East squad in the NBA All Star game. He was tossed out of the game by referee Billy Smith and became the only coach ever ejected from an NBA All Star game. The East lost the game 125-120, and Auerbach's All Star coaching record ended up a not-too-shabby 7-4.

Another area where a lot of interesting trivia and oddities has developed is in cross-sports competition— guys playing pro basketball and also being pros in other sports.

It's a well-publicized fact that Danny Ainge of the Celtics once played for the Toronto Blue Jays. He played but he couldn't hit the curve ball. That's why he's with the Celtics and not with a major league baseball team.

Howie Schultz, who played for a time for the old Brooklyn Dodgers, was the only one I ever heard of to play college basketball and pro baseball at the same time. Back in my Rochester days Del Rice played for a time for the Royals and then played baseball for the Rochester Red Wings before becoming a catcher for the St. Louis Cardinals. There were a couple of other Rochester Royals who made it in other sports. One made it big; the other guy got by. Otto Graham made it big as a great pro football player, while Chuck Connors played a few years with a couple of baseball teams in the majors.

During my playing days with Rochester, Bud Grant played for the Minneapolis Lakers and their owner, Max Winter. When Max bought the Minnesota Vikings football team, Bud went along and became the coach.

Other guys who played both pro basketball and baseball include: Ron Reed, Gene Conley, Bill Sharman, Dick Groat, Frankie Baumholtz and a guy who played for me—Dave DeBusschere, who was also once a pitcher for the Chicago White Sox. Conley was and is the only guy to win championship rings in both sports.

Back in the 1950s, a guy named Clarence "Bevo" Francis, who played for a tiny school named Rio Grande College in southern Ohio, was the talk of the basketball world. All the 6'9" center did was to put the following records in the book:

Most points in a game (113), 1954; most field goals attempted in a game (71), 1954; most field goals made in a game (38), 1954; most free-throws attempted in a game (45), and made (37), 1954; highest scoring average per game (46.5), 1953–54; most games over fifty points in a season (8), 1953–54; and most games over fifty points in a college career (14), 1952–54.

Those records are kind of misleading because Bevo's stats were even more impressive than that. Back in 1953, this kid, named after a popular 1930s soft drink named Beeve, led the Rio Grande Redmen to a 39-0 season. But the college's schedule was looked upon by the National Coach's Association as a weak one. Rio Grande played against a grab-bag mix of junior colleges, seminaries, military bases, and small four-year colleges. The NCAA reinterpreted Bevo's stats, erasing them for all but a dozen games that his team had played. That took away one game where he scored 116 points, and eliminated his 50-point average for the 1952-53 season. It also took away half the games where Bevo scored fifty or more points. All of those take-aways left Bevo and Rio Grande College with something to prove. The guy they called "the common people's All-American" and his tiny Rio Grande College (enrollment–92) suddenly found themselves in great demand during Bevo's sophomore year. Major collegiate powers like Providence, North Carolina State, and Wake Forest—though fifty times Rio Grande's size—scheduled games against Bevo's team. And Bevo, as a sophomore, just went out and strutted his stuff. He scored the most points ever for a single game (113), the second-highest total for a single game (84), and the third-highest total for a single game (82).

With Bevo's basketball heroics Rio Grande College, which was in all kinds of financial difficulties when the 6'9" center arrived on the scene, was able to make the most of his presence. No longer did the players have to get their uniforms washed with their own family laundry. No longer was there a shortage of basketballs. No longer was there a $35 guarantee for games on the road. Now Rio Grande was turning away offers for away games in the low five figures.

They called Bevo Francis "the Legend." And his story was told in newspapers all over America, in magazines, and wherever basketball fans gathered.

With two years of eligibility still left in his collegiate career, Bevo dropped out of Rio Grande College. He needed the money, and no one could blame him for that. But you could only wonder what collegiate scoring records he would have put into the books if he had only played on.

In 1954, when my professional basketball playing career came to an end after I appeared in 51 games for the Milwaukee Hawks, I got to meet Bevo Francis. He was looking for some extra cash and so was I. We spent time together playing on different teams that toured major league baseball parks in the summer when the teams were on the road. Bevo wasn't too swift, but he could shoot the hell out of the ball. After the summer, we went our separate ways. From time to time I heard of him knocking around in basketball's minor leagues trying to pick up a buck. Then he dropped out of sight. A few years back, I got the word that Bevo Francis passed away. He was a national phenomenon at one time. Now he's just a footnote to basketball history. Some people knock his records, saying they were against third-rate teams. But in my book, anyone who could score as many points as Bevo did, no matter who they were against, had to have something on the ball.

4

Family Court

verybody knows about the three DiMaggio brothers in baseball: Joe, Dom, and Vince. Some of you are familiar with the Richard brothers in hockey. Maurice and Henri, and other famous hockey families like the Howes and the Espoisitos. But not too much ink has been given to the basketball genes that have been spread around through the years.

The McGuires, originally out of Far Rockaway, New York, had three of their clan make it with varying degrees of success in basketball. Al McGuire is today the colorful color commentator for college basketball games on network television. Once he was the Marquette University basketball coach who had the distinction of coaching his own son Allie. And once Al played in the same backcourt on the New York Knickerbockers with his brother Dick, the guy I succeeded as coach of the Knicks. They called him "Tricky Dick," and it was a good name because he sure could handle a ball. He was one of the trickiest and smoothest ballhandlers I ever saw. But getting back to Al coaching his son Allie, I remember he got some flak at the time. Some people said the only reason Allie was starting as a sophomore was because his father was the coach. Al handled the criticism in his typically outspoken way. "If I ran a mill," he said, "I wouldn't start my kid sweeping sawdust." When Allie's teammate George "Sugar" Frazier complained he was sitting on the bench while the coach's son started, Al told him, "Sugar, I love my son. For you to start, it has to be a clear knockout. A push goes to Allie."

There was also criticism of a couple of other father-and-son pairings in basketball. Back in 1982, Danny Tarkanian decided to play at UNLV under his father, Coach Jerry Tarkanian. The standard grumblings about nepotism came up. Caught in the middle was Lois Tarkanian, mother of Danny, wife of Jerry. "I think Danny in his heart always wanted to play for his father and the Rebels," she said, . . . "but some of the comments that were made?" In the end it worked out all right. Danny proved to be a pretty good floor leader for Tark's Sharks.

Ray Meyer and his son Joey Meyer at DePaul University also had to handle the flak attack. Joey was the assistant coach on his dad's staff and there were people who grumbled that the kid was there because his father was top dog. But Joey did a hell of a job as a recruiter. Then when Ray retired and Joey took over as head coach at DePaul, the grumblers got going again. But Joey has given the job his best shot and shown that he's got superior coaching ability in his own right.

A collegiate father and son team that didn't get the usual flak treatment was Pete Maravich and his father Press, who was his coach at LSU. From 1967 to 1970,

Pete was a skinny guard with floppy socks performing magic for Louisiana State University. He scored nearly 4,000 points, averaging almost 45 points a game, and went on to become a star in the NBA. The man he left behind at LSU, his father Press, was the one who gave his son the nickname "Pistol Pete." It was Press who taught Pete to shoot the ball fast and often—"like a pistol."

Henry Bibby, a guy on the Knicks who I coached, was part of a famous brother team. Henry played together with his brother Jim on the UCLA championship basketball teams. Jim went on to pitch for a few major league baseball teams while Henry had a pretty good NBA career. I can still remember how excited he was after our Knick team won the 1972–73 championship.

"This is my fourth championship in a row—three with UCLA and now this," he was yelling. "It doesn't get any better than this."

Herb and Larry Brown are probably the most famous of coaching brothers. They grew up in Long Beach, Long Island, where they often played outside on the asphalt court at Central School. Herb went on to play college ball at Vermont while Larry attracted more attention starring at the University of North Carolina as a member of the 1964 United States Olympic team. Some years back the Denver Nuggets coached by Larry and the Detroit Pistons coached by Herb faced each other on an NBA court. It was the first time the brothers had ever coached against each other. "It was probably the only night," said Larry, "where our mother knew exactly where both of us were. At least she was able to see that all the time we spent learning the game as kids on Long Island had paid off."

Bernard and Albert King are a couple of other brothers who grew up in the New York City metropolitan area who went on to make it in the NBA. During their growing-up years Bernard used to give his younger brother Albert tips on how to play the game. When they get together they still talk about their street basketball days on the Brooklyn playgrounds.

It's a real oddity that some of the greatest players never get their sons to fully follow in their footsteps. Hall of Famers George Mikan and Dolph Schayes had sons who went on to play in the NBA. Mikan's brother Ed played six years in the NBA, and his son Larry Mikan played one year with Cleveland. Danny Schayes is a pretty good player for the Milwaukee Bucks, but has nowhere near the ability of his old man. I should know— I played a lot of games and coached a lot of games against Dolph.

Dick and Tom Van Arsdale were not only brothers— they were twins. When I was a scout for the Knicks I checked out the Van Arsdales when they both starred for Indiana University. They played a similar style of basketball and it was difficult telling them apart. Now it can be told—when they played, I watched just one. The other guy never knew the difference.

Until they arrived in the NBA Tom and Dick always played on the same basketball team. Dick was drafted by the Knicks; Tom was drafted by the Detroit Pistons before the 1965–66 season. "When we got out of college a lot of people seemed to think we depended too much on each other on the court and couldn't make it if we were separated," said Tom. "We were happy to prove that we could make it on our own merits."

They did. Dick's career saw him play for better teams than his brother. Tom, who was traded around a lot, remembers, "I always was on teams that lost." Still, Tom gained a lot of respect for his all-around ability. The nice thing about the twins was that they finished their career as they had begun—playing on the same team, the Phoenix Suns.

The record shows that each Van Arsdale played in three NBA All Star games and each scored more than 13,000 points in his career. The record also shows that though they were identical twins, "Tom wound up half an inch taller than me," admitted Dick. "And no one knows when it happened." What everyone knows what happened is that when the Van Arsdales were on the court they gave 100%. They were handy guys to have around.

For a brief space in time there was the memorable and for some touching scene a few years back of a father coaching a professional basketball team that his son played for. That was Coach Bill Van Breda Kolff and son Jan Van Breda Kolff. The older guy had starred at Princeton and NYU and then played for the Knicks in the 1940s, and his kid played for Vanderbilt and lasted nine years in the NBA, mostly as a backup.

Speaking of former Knicks, Ernie Vanderweghe's kid Kiki has made a good name for himself in the NBA. Ernie was born in Montreal, Canada, the son of a semi-professional basketball player. When Ernie was six years old his family moved to Oceanside, New York. After eight high school varsity letters, All American basketball status at Colgate University, medical school, and six seasons with the New York Knickerbockers, Dr. Ernie Vanderweghe made a name for himself. Along the way he even managed to marry a former Miss America, Coleen Kay Hutchins, the sister of former NBA star Mel Hutchins. You might say Kiki has the best of genes: a Miss America for a mother, an uncle who was a great NBA player and a father who was one of the top guards in Knick history.

Players come and go in the NBA, and brother com-
binations do likewise. A few years ago, there seemed to
be a glut of brother acts. Eddie Johnson played for Seattle while his brother Frank was a point guard for the
Washington Bullets. Ray Williams was staging a comeback with the New Jersey Nets and his brother Gus was
finishing up his career with the Atlanta Hawks. Albert
and Bernard King had a chance to see a lot of each other,
too. Albert was on the New Jersey Nets while Bernard
played for the Knicks. And the Paxson brothers, Jim and
John, were with their thing for Portland and Chicago,
respectively. With all the player movement in the NBA,
the only brothers from the 1986–87 season who are still
with the same team are Gerald Wilkins with the Knicks
and Dominique with the Hawks. And don't forget twins
Harvey and Horace Grant of the Bullets and Bulls,
respectively.

One of the most interesting stories involving basketball genes concerns the Jones family of southeastern
Arkansas. Caldwell Jones Sr. and his wife Cecilia had
eight sons. The elder Jones nailed a basketball rim to the
wall of the smokehouse on the family farm. But with
eight active kids jumping and slam-dunking, that setup
didn't last long. So Mr. Jones moved the basket to a
wooden backboard that was attached to a pole set into
the dirt in the middle of the barnyard. That primitive
arrangement proved to be a magnet not only for his children but for kids from miles around.

Caldwell Jones Jr., the sixth of the eight children,
went on to have the most illustrious professional basketball career of the brothers. He began with the San Diego
Conquistadors of the ABA in the '73–74 season. One of
his older brothers, Oliver, was his college coach. Another
older brother, Mel, was drafted by Philadelphia of the

NBA and Denver of the ABA, and played for the Harlem Magicians. Brother Wil was a member of three ABA and two NBA teams. Major Jones had six seasons in the NBA, five of them with the Rockets of Houston. In two of those seasons, Major and Caldwell were teammates on the Rockets. Caldwell's younger brother, Charles, had an outstanding collegiate career at Louisville and still plays in the NBA.

Oliver Caldwell remembers how the Jones family basketball genes were shaped. "During the summer, my brothers and I would play so much basketball that if Daddy needed us for some work, he would have to pick up a switch or a strap and beat us off the court. Caldwell, Wil, and I would usually be one team. I'd play on the inside while they'd play on the outside. That's how we all learned to shoot and work the ball."

5

Nicknames:
from Studebakers to Spud

here are all kinds of odd nicknames in the world of basketball and even odder explanations for where those nicknames came from. Some of the players on the Atlanta Hawks (who used to be the St. Louis Hawks who used to be the Milwaukee Hawks who way back when were coached by yours truly) have some of the most colorful nicknames in the NBA, with some of the most interesting derivations. Anthony "Spud" Webb was given his nickname by a family friend who thought that Spud's head, when he was a baby, resembled the Soviet satellite Sputnik.

Cliff Levingston is called "News" or "House." The first nickname is a short nickname for "Good News," which kind of reflects Levingston's bubbly and outgoing personality. "Brick house" shortencd to "House" is a not-too-complimentary way of calling attention to Cliff's less-than-feathery jumpshot.

"Tree" Rollins picked up his nickname when he was a kid. "The older guys pointed out that I was so tall and thin I was like a young tree. And the name stuck."

Denver's Lafayette Lever didn't get the nickname "Fat" because of his weight. "People think I must have been a fat little kid," he explained. "They expect this chubby guy will come off the bus or the plane, and it takes them by surprise that I'm so skinny. To tell the truth, I got the nickname from my younger brother. He tried to say 'Lafayette' and it came out 'Fat.' The name stuck with me ever since."

Dominique Wilkins is known as the "Human Highlight Film." That nickname is kind of self-explanatory because of all the amazing things Dominique does on a basketball court. He's also called "Nique," a shortening of his first name, and "Zoid," an abbreviated version of "Freakazoid," the title of a song that was once popular.

Glenn "Doc" Rivers picked up his nickname years ago when he walked around all the time in a "Doctor J" t-shirt.

Another guy with an interesting nickname, or should I say nicknames, is Michael Cage. The talented forward is known as "the Enforcer," "Flex," and "Ragin' Cajun." A native of Arkansas, Cage found out a couple of years ago through an uncle that he was of Cherokee descent. Michael also learned that his grandfather lived on a reservation in Kansas and was known as "Chief Flying Cloud." So the newest nickname for the L.A. Clipper star is "Flying Cloud."

There's a lot of history involved with the way teams in the NBA got their names. And although some clubs have moved from city to city, they've kept the original nicknames they started out with.

The Knicks and the Celtics are the only two teams still playing in the NBA in their original cities. The name "Knickerbockers" comes from when New York was New Amsterdam, and the city's Dutch settlers wore knickers—trousers that were bunched up at the knees. The name "Celtics" was given to the team in 1946 by Walter Brown, the founder of the franchise. "We'll call them the Boston Celtics," he said. "The name has a great basketball tradition especially when you think of the original 'Celtics' team. Boston is full of Irishmen, so we'll put the players in green uniforms and call them the Boston Celtics after their Celtic ancestors." Both the Knicks and Celtics have been going after each other under the same name since 1946.

The Atlanta Hawks were once the St. Louis Hawks, and before that, they were the Milwaukee Hawks. Before that, in 1948, they were the Tri-Cities Blackhawks. The three cities refer to Moline, Illinois; Rock Island, Illinois; and Davenport, Iowa. Way back in 1831, the Blackhawk War was fought in that tri-cities area. And that's how the original Blackhawks nickname, now shortened to Hawks, came to be.

My old team, the Rochester Royals, played in the NBA for nine seasons and then was transferred to Cincinnati. The Royals nickname was kept. Then, in 1972, the franchise shifted to Kansas City, Missouri, and with that shift, the Royals' nickname was dropped. It wasn't really a slight toward the old Rochester-Cincinnati tradition. It was to avoid confusion. In the Kansas City area, there were already two teams with the Royals' nickname—the Kansas City and Omaha baseball teams. The new nickname for the basketball franchise was the Kansas City-Omaha Kings. They became the

Kansas City Kings in '75, and when the franchise moved
to Sacramento a decade later, the nickname Kings went
along with them. I always had a soft spot in my heart for
the Royals nickname and thought that was a perfect opportunity for it to be reborn. But I guess it wasn't to be.

Not too many people know that the Denver Nuggets
were charter members of the NBA. But that team didn't
last too long—just one season. When the Denver Rockets
of the ABA came into the NBA, they were forced to
change their name because the Houston Rockets team
was doing its thing. The management there decided to
rename the Denver franchise with the same nickname of
the original NBA team. "Nuggets" is a word that goes
back more than a century to a time when gold and silver
mining was booming in Colorado.

Charlotte, Miami, Minnesota, and Orlando are the
four newest NBA franchises. And all of them have interesting stories on how they got their nicknames. Originally, the Charlotte team was nicknamed the Charlotte
Spirit. But that didn't go over too well, and it was
dropped. A big contest was launched among the fans to
come up with a name for the team. Runner-up names
included: the Charlotte Gold, the Charlotte Knights,
and somehow the original nickname, the Charlotte
Spirit. You all know what the winning name was: the
Charlotte Hornets. This makes the third time that a
sports team in the city of Charlotte has been given that
name. A World Football League club and a Minnesota
Twins baseball farm team both were once called the
Charlotte Hornets.

General partner Zev Bufman explained how Miami
decided on its nickname. "The heat was it. The owners
just felt it represented the area. When you think of
Miami, that's what you think of." Although the Miami

franchise received more than 5,000 entries in a "Name the Team" contest that included such candidates as Palm Trees, Beaches, Suntan, and Shade, the Heat beat them all out.

In 1987, after receiving 6,000 entries to name their team, the choice for the Minnesota franchise came down to Timberwolves vs. Polars. Timberwolves easily won. That animal is native to Minnesota, and no other pro sports team has ever used it.

The *Orlando Sentinel* sponsored a "Name the Team" contest in that city. Just like with Minnesota, the competition came down to two names: Magic and Juice. Orlando general manager Pat Williams explained how Magic became the winning name. "Magic is synonymous with the Orlando area. We are the tourist capital of the world. We have the Magic Kingdom and Disneyworld. The tourism slogan here is 'Come to the magic.'"

Some people think that the Chicago Bulls got their name because of the stockyards in that city. But that's not the case. They were named the Bulls in 1966 by their first owner, Richard Klein, who thought it was a good nickname for a team. Some people say that Klein admired bulls because of their toughness and looked forward to having a team that had that same quality.

The Pistons came into being in 1948 and were known then as the Ft. Wayne Zollner Pistons. It was a case of an owner naming a team for himself and for the business that he ran. Fred Zollner owned a big piston-manufacturing company. In 1957, the team moved to Detroit. And the nickname Pistons moved right along with it.

Way back in 1925, there was a Philadelphia Warriors team in the American Basketball League. In 1946, when Philadelphia joined the NBA, it took its nickname from

that old team. Many years and many miles later, the
Golden State Warriors are a descendant of the old Philadelphia Warriors. They've gone through a couple of geographical shifts. Philadelphia became the San Francisco
Warriors, San Francisco became the Oakland Warriors,
and Oakland became the Golden State Warriors.

A couple of years ago, a newspaper guy came up with
the idea of teams trading nicknames. The suggestion had
some merit, but it was no dice. The guy's thought was
that the Utah Jazz become the Utah Lakers and the Los
Angeles Lakers become the Los Angeles Jazz. Actually,
both Utah and Los Angeles have team nicknames from
cities both franchises left. Utah came into being in 1979
when the New Orleans Jazz moved there. That New Orleans basketball team is only a memory, but the Utah Jazz
kept its nickname and team colors. The Minneapolis
Lakers made the move to Los Angeles before the 1960
season and took with it its nickname that comes from the
state of Minnesota's motto: "the land of 10,000 lakes."
I don't know of too many lakes in L.A. or too much jazz
in Utah. Maybe that newspaper guy had a good idea
after all.

The three NBA Texas teams all have interesting stories behind their nicknames. The Houston Rockets were
once the San Diego Rockets. The nickname has suited
both franchises—both San Diego and Houston are famous for housing space programs and industries. The
San Antonio Spurs got their name in a public naming
contest. It's one of my favorite team nicknames—short,
to the point, and it's a word that makes you think of
Texas. The team is actually a descendant of the old Dallas Chaparrals of the ABA. But when the Chaps moved in
1973 to San Antonio, their nickname became a footnote
to history. The Dallas Mavericks came into being in

1980. A contest was conducted by a Dallas radio station, and the team's executives, after sorting out the suggested names, picked Mavericks because they thought that it would underscore the Texan flavor of the franchise.

Not too many people remember that back in 1963, the old Syracuse Nats were sold and became the Philadelphia 76ers. Anybody who knows his history knows how Philly got its nickname.

In 1968, the new Phoenix franchise sponsored a name-the-team contest among its fans, offering a cash prize and a couple of season tickets to the winner. The Phoenix Suns beat out such nicknames as Scorpions, Rattlers, and Dust Devils to become the official nickname of the club.

The Portland Trail Blazers were founded in 1970 and also got their nickname through a "Name the Team" contest. Nearly 200 people had the same idea for the nickname. Harry Glickman, the guy who founded the Portland team, said at the time, "We are delighted with the name Trail Blazers. It reflects both the ruggedness of the Pacific Northwest and the start of a major league era in our state." I was coaching the Knicks in Portland in 1970 when they announced the nickname of the team, and you could see it was one of those names that everyone liked.

The New Jersey Nets began life in the ABA and were known as the New Jersey Americans. In 1968, the team left Jersey and moved to Commack, Long Island. It was re-named the New York Nets. The reasoning was that since the New York metropolitan area had the football Jets and the baseball Mets, why not the basketball Nets? The odd thing about the team is that before the '77–78 season, it jumped back across the Hudson River again to New Jersey. Some people thought it would go back to its original name, the New Jersey Americans. But the nickname Nets moved along with the team.

A guy named R.D. Treblicox of Whitefish Bay, Wisconsin, won himself a brand-new car and a place in *Holzman on Hoops* for coining the nickname for the Milwaukee Bucks. R.D.'s winning entry, back in 1968, beat out other suggested names like Stags, Skunks, and Stallions. "Bucks are spirited, good jumpers, fast, and agile," said R.D. "These are exceptional qualities for basketball players." That Treblicox guy knew his nicknames and knew his basketball.

Alliteration was probably one of the reasons for the name Cavaliers winning out over the competition in a Cleveland newspaper contest back in 1970. But that name in recent years has been de-emphasized in favor of "Cavs." I guess the owners of the Cleveland team and the media think that the team's formal nickname is a little too fancy for an NBA club.

When the Indiana franchise came into being in 1967 in the ABA, the owners said the nickname was picked because they intended to set the pace in professional basketball. That's how the nickname Pacers came to be. It stayed with the team when it joined the NBA in 1976.

The Washington Bullets' nickname goes all the way back to the old Baltimore Bullets basketball team that first got started in 1946. That Baltimore club picked up its nickname because it played its games near a foundry that made ammunition during World War II. You'd need a road map to follow the evolution of nicknames for that franchise. That original Baltimore team disbanded after a few years. A second Baltimore team came into being in 1963 and was named the Bullets after the original team. A decade later, that franchise shifted to Washington, D.C., and some of you may remember it was re-named the Capitol Bullets. That name didn't make too big a hit. In 1974, Washington Bullets became the name of the franchise. I guess if the guys wanted to be geographically accurate, they would have called themselves the Landover Bullets because the arena they play in is in Landover, Maryland.

If you've read this far in my team nickname section, you probably realize that a lot of screwy situations have come to pass what with franchise shifts and new owner-ships and the birth of new teams and popularity contests deciding what a club should be called. In my book, and this is my book, one of the oddest nickname situations involves the Los Angeles Clippers. You may have to read this explanation twice. The Los Angeles Clippers, if you want to be technical, were once upon a time the Buffalo Braves. Here's what happened. In 1971, the City of San Diego lost its NBA franchise when its team moved to Houston and became the Rockets. In 1978, the Buffalo Braves moved to San Diego. The owners thought that San Diego Braves just wouldn't do as a nickname. So one of those famous "Name-the-Team" contests was held. Lots of beautiful clipper ships once passed through the great harbor of San Diego. So the winning entry, the of-ficials decided, was the Clippers. I don't think there were ever any clipper ships in Los Angeles. But in 1984, when the franchise shifted from San Diego to Los Ange-les, the nickname Clippers stayed with it. Whew!

The location of a huge Boeing aircraft plant in Seat-tle was the inspiration for Howard E. Schmidt's sug-gestion of Supersonics as a nickname back in 1967 for the Seattle NBA franchise. Mr. Schmidt got a free trip to Palm Springs, California, and season tickets for Seattle's first basketball season, and the franchise got itself a nice space-age nickname.

If you got worn out reading this section, I got worn out writing it. But all we covered were the NBA teams. There are plenty of other stories behind pro basketball nicknames. The Chicago Studebakers, for example, were a team in the old NBL that was purchased by the United Auto Workers Union of a Chicago-based Studebaker plant. And then there were teams like the Sheboygan Redskins, the Akron Firestones, the Cleveland Rosenblums, the Whiting All-Americans, the Warren Penn Oilers, and the Chicago Gears. How those team names came to be, though, is a subject for another book. Doing this section on names somehow reminded me of the time I was scouting a kid from Czechoslovakia. We decided to give him a vision test. I got hold of an eye chart and told the kid, "All right, let's hear you read the bottom line."

"Read the bottom line?" he said. "I know him."

And so much for names.

Dr. James Naismith, who invented the game of basketball in 1891.

The Buffalo Germans, one of basketball's early legendary teams. Over 30 years they won 792 games and lost just 86. *Front row:* Redlein and Rohde. *Middle row:* Faust, Heerdt (captain), and Miller. *Back Row:* Maier and Burkhardt.

Forrest "Phog" Allen, longtime University of Kansas coach. He once played and coached for the Buffalo Germans.

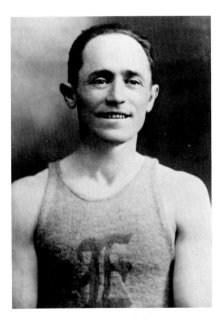

Barney Sedran, one of the great pro players of the teens and twenties. He was small (5'4") but extremely quick and teamed with Nat Holman on the great New York Whirlwinds.

After starring with the New York Whirlwinds, guard Nat Holman, one of the game's great passers, joined the Original Celtics.

A gallery of the Original Celtics: Pete Barry played for the New York Celtics (the descendants of the Original Celtics) before WWI, and remained an excellent pro player through the early '30s.

John Beckman was a great shooter and the outstanding player of the '20s.

Joe Lapchick was one of the game's first big men.

Dutch Dehnert was the inventor of the pivot play.

Senda Berenson Abbot, the "Mother of Women's Basketball." While at Smith College she wrote the special rules for women's basketball that remained in effect for 75 years.

Lynette Woodward (*right*) became the first female Harlem Globetrotter in 1985.

Ann Meyers, the first woman to sign a contract with an NBA team.

The Harlem Rens, the best barnstorming team of the '30s. *Left to right:* Clarence "Fat" Jenkins, Bill Yancey, John Holt, James "Pappy" Ricks, Eyre "Bruiser" Saitch, Charles "Tarzan" Cooper, and "Wee" Willie Smith.

At 5'7", Harold "Fat" Jenkins was billed as "the fastest man in basketball."

Joe Lapchick called 6'4" Charles "Tarzan" Cooper "the best center I ever saw."

The acquisition of 6'5" "Wee" Willie Smith in 1932 made the Rens almost unbeatable; in a 4-year period beginning that year, the Rens won 473 games and lost only 49.

William "Pop" Gates joined the Rens in 1939, when they went 112-7 and won the World Professional Championship held in Chicago. He later played for the Harlem Globetrotters.

In 1950, Charles Cooper of Duquesne University became the first black player drafted into the NBA.

The same season, Nat "Sweetwater" Clifton left the Globetrotters to play for the New York Knicks. Here he shows off his reach for Knick coach Joe Lapchick.

The Harlem Globetrotters'
Marques Haynes was one of the
greatest dribblers ever.

Bob Kurland, a 7-footer from
Oklahoma A&M, was the center on
both the 1948 and 1952 U.S.
Olympic teams.

The 1956 U.S. Olympic team was a scoring powerhouse; their average
margin of victory was 30 points. Players only: (*front row*) Ron Tomsic, Bill
Evans, K.C. Jones, Carl Cain, Gib Ford and Bob Jeangerard; (*back row*) Bill
Houghland, Chuck Darling, Bill Russell, Dick Boushka, Burdie Haldorson,
and Jim Walsh.

Dave Cowens was a scrappy 6'9" center for the
Boston Celtics for 10 years. He was selected to 7
All-Star games, and was NBA MVP in 1973.

Arnold "Red" Auerbach, the great
Boston Celtics coach, became the
only coach ever thrown out of an
NBA All-Star game in 1967.

In 1949, Al Cervi was the only man
ever to be named Coach of the
Year and Most Valuable Player in
the same year.

During the '70s, "Pistol" Pete Maravich was an NBA scoring machine. He was coached by his father, Press Maravich, at Louisiana State, where he averaged almost 45 points a game from 1967 to 1970.

Bernard King is the better player (averaging over 22 points a game in his 13-year career) . . .

. . . but little brother Albert was a solid NBA contributor during most of the 1980s.

Dick Van Arsdale played for better NBA teams . . .

. . . but twin brother Tom was half an inch taller. They both played in 3 All-Star games and each scored more than 14,000 points in his career.

Rick Barry is the
only player to
lead both the
ABA and NBA
in scoring (NBA,
1967; ABA,
1969).

High-scoring
Connie Hawkins
played in the
old ABL, for the
Harlem Globe-
trotters, in the
ABA, and the
NBA.

Mike Riordan was a hardworking overachiever who wasn't even drafted—he was a supplemental pick by the Knicks after the 1967 draft. He later became a good scorer for the Bullets.

Bob Pettit, a 6'9" power forward, was the first NBA player to score more than 20,000 points. He was a great offensive rebounder.

George Mikan, at 6'10" and 255 pounds, was the first franchise player in NBA history. He led the Lakers to 5 NBA titles.

Elgin Baylor was one of the great scorers of all time, and the first NBA player to display the stylish razzle-dazzle that is taken for granted today.

At 5'7" and 135 pounds, Spud Webb constantly amazes with his quickness, ballhandling, and jumping ability. His hard work has made him a starter for the Atlanta Hawks.

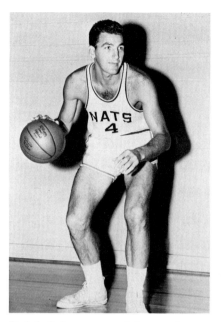

Dolph Schayes was nicknamed "The Rainbow Kid" because of the high arch he had on his outside shots.

"Mr. Clutch," Jerry West, was one of the greatest shooting guards in NBA history; he averaged 27 points a game in 14 seasons as a Laker.

Julius Erving was one of the greatest showmen in NBA history, and one of only three players to score 30,000 points in their careers.

Bill Laimbeer was the 65th pick in the 1979 NBA draft, but that didn't stop him from becoming a four-time All Star and one of the leading rebounders in the league for a decade.

John Havlicek was the greatest non-starter in NBA history, and the best shooting, jumping, rebounding, passing, ballhandling, defending forward-guard of his era.

Bill Russell led the Boston Celtics to 11 NBA titles in 13 years, and was named MVP five times. He was the fiercest defender the game has ever known.

"The Big Dipper," Wilt Chamberlain, averaged 30 points a game over a 14-year career. In 1961–62, he averaged 50 points a game, and in one game that season scored 100 points.

Willis Reed led the Knicks to NBA titles in 1970 and 1973. He is the only player to be selected as MVP for the season, the All-Star Game, and the playoffs in the same season (1970).

Kareem Abdul-Jabbar is the all-time leading scorer in NBA history, and was named MVP a record 6 times in his 20-year career.

Larry Bird is one of the greatest clutch players in NBA history. He's a three-time MVP and a consummate team player.

Magic Johnson is another three-time MVP. One of the finest passers the game has ever seen, he led the Lakers to 5 titles in the '80s.

Michael Jordan, the greatest one-on-one player ever, is also an excellent passer and defender. But it's his innovative scoring moves that draw the crowds.

Along with Hakeem Olajuwon and David Robinson, Patrick Ewing is one of the three best centers in the game today. Here he releases his soft-touch shot over the outstretched arm of Jack Sikma.

6

My Favorite Lines

eader's Digest always has a section of "quotable quotes." I've picked up my share of stories over the years. I don't know if they'd make *Readers' Digest* but they did make their way into this book. They kind of give some insight into the hardwood humor of basketball.

When Mel Counts was just a sophomore and put his Oregon State team into the 1962 NCAA regionals, his coach reached to praise the seven footer. "He's so good," he said, "that you could cut Mel in two and he'd make a pair of darn good guards."

Back around the same time, a tough time for the New York Knickerbockers, Eddie Donovan, then the coach, got off one of his better lines. Trainer Don Fredericks pulled a tendon in his wrists while bowling. "Don, you now have picked up the occupational hazard in pro basketball," Donovan smiled. "Unwillingness to give up the ball."

Going into the 1988–89 season, the Utah Jazz weighed in as the heaviest team in the NBA—they averaged 224.33 pounds per player. Their portly coach, Frank Layden, cracked, "And that doesn't even include me."

Guys like Ron Luciano and Joe Garagiola have made the point over and over again that baseball is a funny game with a lot of characters in it. Well, basketball is, too. All kinds of oddballs, interesting types, and guys with a gift of gab have been involved with the sport.

Mychal Thompson, the backup center of the Los Angeles Lakers, has made it perfectly clear that one day he hopes to be the Prime Minister of the Bahamas, his homeland. The way he uses language, it seems to me that he has a good shot at the job.

After the Lakers beat Dallas 119–102 in Game 5 of the 1987–1988 Western Conference Finals, Thompson said: "We played like a wife's divorce lawyer. We went after everything." A while before that he was asked why he named his newborn son Mychel.

Thompson's response was, "I didn't want him to have the burden of having to live up to my name."

Kurt Nimphius is a player that the press has a lot of fun with, but he seems to have a lot of fun with them, too. When he was traded a couple of years ago from the Pistons to the Clippers, he left his Porsche behind but took his pet cockatoos Sufi and Sheva with him. "They're good friends," explained Nimphius. "And you don't have to walk them. They don't need shots. They're perfect for someone like me."

A lovable oddball, Nimphius explains, "The press likes to pick on me, make up stuff that makes me look weird just to get a good story. I've been misquoted a lot.

Hey. I'm weird enough without people making up stories."

Chuck Connors was one of the true all-time characters, and one who made a living out of his outgoing ways. On November 5, 1946, in the Celtic's first game, Connors took a two-handed set shot and shattered the glass backboard at the west end of Boston Arena. The game was delayed for an hour. Even before that Connors always wanted to be a smash.

I played with him back in my Rochester Royal days and even then everyone knew that he was headed somehow for a career in show business. Chuck loved to do handstands on the basketball court and mimic the refs. But his favorite routine was a loud version of "Casey at the Bat." In hotels, on buses and trains, in locker rooms, Chuck would emote his special version of that old classic.

"I want to be an actor," he would explain. "You guys have nothing better to do than be an audience." We would complain that we had heard enough, but Chuck would go on with his recitation. "I need the practice," he'd say. He did, but our ears needed a rest. I guess that practice did him some good. For Chuck Connors went on to do *The Rifleman* and other movie and TV roles. And to think we helped him get his start.

One of the funniest guys I scouted was Tom Hoover, who played for the Knicks from 1963 to 1965. He was 6'9" and 230 pounds and always full of stories. Unlike many basketball players, he was a pretty good fighter. Tom loved to tell about the time he got into some trouble while playing in the Pan Am games and spent a day in a Mexican jail.

The authorities arrested him on some minor charge and kept moving him from jail to jail, but they could never find one big enough for him. Finally, they moved him into an outdoor jail. It had no roof and high walls.

There was a little guy in the jail with Tom. "*Señor,*" the guy pleaded, "you pick me up and throw me over the wall so I can escape." Hoover did what the guy wanted but he claimed it took him three shots to get the guy out of there.

When Tom joined the Knicks he would always come over to me and say, "Coach, dress me up." That meant he wanted me to loan him a few dollars. I was only a scout and probably making less than him but "Hoov" was such an agreeable guy that I would ask him how much he wanted.

"Lend me fifty."

"All I got is twenty."

"I'll take it."

I would give Hoover the twenty knowing I'd never see it again, but I figured I made thirty dollars on the original negotiations.

George Glamack was a guy who played at North Carolina and was a Helms Foundation award winner. He was 6'5" and our first center with the Rochester Royals. George got a lot of mileage out of his great hook shot.

Our nickname for him was "the Blind Bomber." For even though he wore glasses, he was always squinting, and he couldn't see from one end of the court to the other.

Every game George would yell "Red, Red, what's the score." He could never read the score because of his poor eyesight. No matter what the score was I'd tell him we were down by five points or eight points.

"You sure, Red?" he would yell back.

"Yeah, George. Dig in some more."

It wasn't really so much lying on my part as it was giving George extra incentive to play harder.

The coaching fraternity has had a lot of characters. Many of them have not only known the game and had great success, but they also have had a way with words and they've been involved in strange happenings. Sometimes the things they've said weren't really intended to be funny. But they've just come out that way. Once, when I was coaching the Knicks, there was one game when we did much better the second half of the game than we did in the first. A reporter asked me how come. "How the hell should I know?" was my response. The media thought my one-liner was hilarious. But all I was trying to do was be honest. I guess that's happened to a lot of other guys, too.

When Al McGuire was coaching Marquette, he said "I can do two things in life—coach basketball and tend bar. I'm fighting to keep the apron off."

Frank Layden got off a lot of great lines as the coach of the Utah Jazz. But one of his more interesting comments was from his days as assistant coach with the Atlanta Hawks. "We got a pretty good reading on this fellow who just joined our team when he filled out the information sheet for our Public Relations Department. On the line where 'church preference' was requested, the guy wrote 'red brick.'"

Johnny Bach, who had all those great years coaching Fordham, used to wince every time he talked about the home-court edge some teams enjoyed. Once he brought his team to a midwestern college—a place where the home court edge was a thing of pride. The lights were dim but Bach's guys played their hearts out. As the game moved along the lights got even dimmer.

"I can't see the scoreboard," Bach told one of the officials. "How much time is there left to play? What's the score?"

The ref looked right into Bach's face. "There's just one minute left to play," he said. "And we're ahead by four points."

Harley "Skeeter" Swift was a journeyman player in the American Basketball Association. The guy always felt neglected. (I haven't neglected him.) He always complained to the media. "I don't care what you write. Give me some ink. Can't I be on some all-star team? I don't care if it's the all-ugly team. Anything. Let me know I'm around."

Back in 1964, Horace "Bones" McKinney, an ordained Baptist minister, was coaching Wake Forest against Princeton in a holiday basketball tournament. McKinney was an excitable type. He kicked at the air with so much force that his shoe flew off and landed in the middle of the court. Running out on the floor to get his shoe back, Bones bent down and his fountain pen fell out of his jacket. He was working fast to get his shoe and his fountain pen, and when he gathered them and himself up, he looked up and saw the whole Princeton team coming at him on a fast break. Bones explained: "I did the only thing I could. I threw up my hands and started playing defense."

Some real startling oddities have taken place in the world of coaching. Bud Grant played for the Minneapolis Lakers from 1949 to '51 but never coached in the NBA. Two decades later, Grant was coaching another Minnesota team, the Vikings, in the Super Bowl in 1970, 1974, 1975, and 1977.

Then there's Charlie Eckman. One of the great characters of the game, Charlie has the rare distinction of having appeared in the NBA Championship Final Series two straight seasons without playing for any of the teams involved. In 1954 he was a ref in the Finals between Minneapolis and Syracuse. The following year he coached the Fort Wayne Pistons against Syracuse in the Finals.

But Layden, tops the list of those who are great with one-liners. A Layden sampler includes:

"I didn't hire my son Scott as an assistant coach because he's my son. I hired him because I'm married to his mother."

A couple of years back, Layden's Utah Jazz team had heavyweights Mel Turpin, Darryl Dawkins, Mark Eaton, and Karl Malone. The portly Layden remarked, "Having all those guys on the team gave us a lot of balance on the bench. I've been tilting it when I sit down. But if we keep one on the end, a couple in the middle, and me on my end, we should be all right."

Layden has also been the subject of some interesting one-liners. For a few years now, people have been trying to put some weight on the 7'6", 205-pound Manute Bol. One wit suggested that Bol spend the summer with Layden.

Somehow, whenever Bol is mentioned, the subject of food seems to come up. When World B. Free heard that Bol's first NBA basket was on a pick-and-roll, Free said, "Hmmmm, it must have been a toothpick-and-roll." And Woody Allen recently observed that Bol was so skinny that he didn't have to travel with the rest of the team— "they can just fax him to the next city."

7

The Wild and Woolly ABA

red, white, and blue basketball, a three-point field goal for shots from twenty-five feet or more, George Mikan as the first commissioner and Dave DeBusschere as its last commissioner, owners like Charles O. Finley (who once owned the Oakland Athletics), and coaches like Al Bianchi, Wilt Chamberlain, Slater Martin, Jim Pollard, Max Zaslofsky— all of that was just part of the story of the American Basketball Association.

It was a league where the average ticket price was four dollars and students were admitted for a dollar or less. It was a league of regional franchises: the Carolina Cougars playing to the fans of Greensboro, Charlotte, and Raleigh; the Texas Chaparrals and their fans in Dallas, Ft. Worth, and Lubbock; the Floridians, with a population rooting for them that came from Miami Beach, West Palm Beach, Tampa, and Jacksonville; and the Virginia Squires, whose region covered Norfolk, Hampton Road, Roanoke, and Richmond.

The forerunner of the ABA was the American Basketball League that was organized in 1961 by Abe Saperstein, owner of the Harlem Globetrotters. Abe served as the commissioner and had teams in Cleveland, Pittsburgh, Chicago, Washington, Kansas City, Los Angeles, San Francisco, and Hawaii. The ABL had a three-point goal for shots made from thirty feet out or more and a split season—the first-half champion played the second-half champion in divisional finals before moving on to the championship finals. The ABL also had Connie Hawkins, a great shooter and drawing card, who was banned by the NBA because he allegedly was involved with gamblers.

The ABL lasted through only two seasons, but it showed potential for a rival league to the NBA. In 1967 the American Basketball Association was created. A war began between the NBA and the ABA. Rick Barry jumped leagues and became a member of the Oakland franchise in the ABA, a team owned by singer Pat Boone. Connie "The Hawk" Hawkins signed with the ABA and averaged almost 27 points a game to become the first scoring leader in that league's history. The way he played, the fact that he was getting a second chance at the pro game kind of made him a symbol of the ABA. Spencer Haywood signed with Denver in the ABA as a "hardship case," and Zelmo Beatty jumped from the NBA to the ABA. Four NBA refs also moved over to the new league. That league had many top players who went on to make a name for themselves in the NBA: Maurice Lucas, Moses Malone, Dan Issel, Artis Gilmore, David Thompson, George McGinnis, Bobby Jones, George Gervin, and especially Julius Erving.

Characters aplenty dotted the ABA. There was the owner of the Pittsburgh franchise, Gabe Rubin, a guy who made trades and didn't bother to tell his coaches about them until the deals were done. He went after Art Heyman, then told reporters: "No, I didn't trade for Art because he's Jewish. I traded for him because I'm Jewish." Ned Doyle, founder of the advertising firm Doyle, Dane and Bernbach, was questioned as to why he put up money for the Miami Floridians. "The Brooklyn Bridge," he smiled, "wasn't for sale."

Wendell Lardner died a few years back in a plane crash near JFK airport. But he was a free spirit when he was in the ABA. Wendell was the only player in the ABA to ask for four single complimentary tickets in four different sections of arenas—to please four different girlfriends.

There were some great coaches in the ABA, guys who went on to make it big in the NBA—K.C. Jones, Hubie Brown, Al Bianchi, Stan Albeck. Refs who worked in the NBA included Norm Drucker, Jack Madden, Jess Kersey, Earl Strom, and John Vanak. Two players made full-circle jumps—NBA to ABA to NBA—Rick Barry and Billy Cunningham.

Maybe it was because that league struggled for an identity, but it seemed to me that they had the best players' nicknames: Charles "Helicopter" Heinz, George "Machine Gun" Thompson, Les "Big Game" Hunter, Mack "The Knife" Calvin, Ira "The Large" Harge, Levern "Jelly Tart" Roland.

For all those who followed the ABA through all its struggles and high moments there were a lot of thrills. There was always a lot of suspense wondering what teams would survive, what new players would be coming in, and when the NBA would finally win its "war."

After the 1975–76 season both leagues agreed on a merger. Four ABA teams were taken into the NBA: the New York Nets, Denver Nuggets, Indiana Pacers, and San Antonio Spurs. The players of the three other existing ABA teams were dispersed around the NBA. And that was the end of the American Basketball Association.

One of the footnotes to ABA history was the red, white, and blue basketball. Alex Hannum coached in the ABA and didn't like the basketball. "It belongs on the nose of a seal," he said. "I never went that far in my dislike for it, but I didn't like it either. The rotating colors I always thought were a distraction. The ball was exciting for the ABA and that's what that league tried to do— always generate excitement."

There were many people in the NBA who looked at the ABA as some kind of inflated league, but I told those guys that if you take these ABA teams and players lightly, you're gonna get shocked. They're going to murder you. It turned out to be true . . . the ABA was competitive, with a lot of great players. The only real thing the NBA had over them was that we were in business longer.

8

Cinderfellas

ne of the great things about the NBA is all the "Cinderfella" stories—guys who came in unheralded and made something of themselves. Scouts claimed the players would never stick in the NBA. Not only have these players stuck, they have gone on to become pretty good ballplayers. For a lot of them it hasn't been easy—they've been passed along from team to team, but they've never given up. Those are my kind of players.

Michael Adams of the Denver Nuggets is one of those players. In high school he never even dreamed of playing in the NBA. He was one of nine children and knew he had no shot at even attending college without a basketball scholarship. Although he had an outstanding high school career in Hartford, Connecticut, no major colleges offered him a scholarship on national signing day.

"Fortunately," Adams says, "I was too young then to let that bother me." Fortunately,

Boston College came through for Michael, but only after he graduated from high school.

Adams did pretty well in college, averaging nearly 15 points a game. But in the 1985 NBA draft he was a low pick—65th, in the third round, by the Sacramento Kings.

"I think the shorter guys, Muggsy Bogues, Spud Webb, and myself," the 5′11″ Adams says, "have assets that are overlooked. We can outrun the bigger people and it's a problem for them to defend against us. But some scouts don't see it that way."

The Sacramento Kings didn't see it that way, either. They released Adams after a couple of months had passed in the 1985–86 season. And the revolving door started revolving for Adams. He was picked up by Washington, who released him twice. In between there was a stint for Adams in the Continental Basketball Association with the Bay State Bombardiers. Adams made his mark in the CBA, winning the Rookie of the Year award and being named to the All Star second team.

In November of '86, Washington signed him again. Then, in the 1987–88 season, the Bullets traded Adams along with Jay Vincent to Denver for guard Darrell Walker and forward Mark Alarie. That proved to be just the break Adams needed.

"When I first got traded, I felt a little animosity," Adams said. "Then the trade turned out to be a blessing in disguise for me." It was also a blessing for the Nuggets.

With the encouragement of Denver Coach Doug Moe, Adams, always a playmaker first, began to work on his outside shot. "I increased my shooting range by five feet and just kept shooting, trying to improve my jump shot," said Adams. The shots started to fall.

On March 17, 1988, Adams hit a three-pointer against the Portland Trail Blazers that broke Danny Ainge's previous NBA record of 23 consecutive games of making at least one three-point shot. From its start on January 28 the streak moved to 43 games and April 23 before it was stopped.

There was always pressure on Adams just to survive in the NBA, so he handled the pressure of the three-point streak pretty well. "I never went into a game feeling I had to make a three-pointer to keep the streak going," Adams said. "I went into a game planning to win. If we had a large lead at the end of a game and I needed a three, I'd shoot a few. Otherwise I wouldn't look for them in a close game just to keep the streak going."

Adams is just one of the 25% of the players in the NBA who were not first- or second-round picks. That says a little bit about how tough it is for a guy drafted in the third round or below to make it. But they do.

Michael Cooper of the Lakers was picked out of the University of New Mexico in the third round, the 60th pick, in 1978. Some said he couldn't shoot, that he was too thin at 6'7" and 176 pounds. All Cooper did was become one of the leaguer's best defensive players and a fine three-point shooter.

"When you're a late-round selection," Cooper says, "you have to be very, very special as far as working your butt off and playing hard."

Jim Petersen of the Golden State Warriors is another Cinderfella story. Drafted as the 51st pick in the third round in 1984 out of the University of Minnesota, Petersen notes, "I wasn't supposed to have a chance. My college coach, Jim Dutcher, didn't give me a chance. He had already sent me off to Europe.

"Nobody knew who I was. That's one of the first questions Hakeem Olajuwon asked: 'Who's Jim Petersen?' I had a good rookie camp and the Houston Rockets offered me a guaranteed contract, which gave me all the confidence in the world. Houston turned out to be a great opportunity for me. I was in the right place at the right time."

Nobody still knew Petersen's name even though he was on the Houston roster. "Up until the playoffs and NBA Finals in 1986," Petersen admits, "I was pretty much a nobody. But then I thought I gained a lot of respect."

Working with weights, Petersen built himself up, and his play also got better. Today, at 6'10" and 215 pounds, Petersen is one of the more powerful forwards in the NBA. And everybody knows who he is.

One of the biggest success stories in the NBA is Mark Eaton, the 7'5" center on the Utah Jazz. As a senior at UCLA, he played a grand total of 41 minutes. "The scouts wrote me off," he admits.

"I had watched the NBA on TV," he continued, "and I felt I could be a backup center. I just wanted the opportunity I never got at UCLA."

In 1979, Eaton was drafted by Phoenix in the fifth round—the 107th pick. He was eligible for the draft because he was out of school three seasons between high school and college and his college class graduated in 1979. He never played a minute for Phoenix.

Then, in 1982, Utah picked him in the fourth round—the 72nd pick. To look at the guy, a lumbering Goliath out there, it seemed he had no chance to stick in the NBA. But Frank Layden and the other people on the Jazz worked a great deal with him. And Eaton busted his chops. Midway through his rookie season of 1982–83, he moved into the Jazz's starting lineup.

"All of a sudden I was playing against guys I had been watching on TV my whole life," says Eaton. "I remember at first looking around and thinking, 'What am I doing out here?' But you get over that pretty quickly and then you have to work pretty hard to establish the respect of the other players. But really, that's the easy part. The hard part is getting a chance and making it. Not many fourth-round picks are playing in the NBA, so I feel pretty fortunate to be where I am."

And the Jazz are lucky to have him. Four times he's led the NBA in blocked shots; one of those years, 1986, Eaton set the record for the most blocked shots in a season. At first he was just a banger, a blocker, a rebounder. Now he's added some offense to his game. There's just no telling how good the big lug is going to be.

Bill Laimbeer of the Detroit Pistons is another guy I'd put on my "all-Cinderfella" team. He was born on May 19, 1957, in Boston, but you'd never know it the way he gets up for the Celtics. You'd also never know how much knocking around he did before he found a home with the Pistons.

Even in college Laimbeer knocked around. He played as a freshman for Notre Dame, then transferred to Owens Tech. He never played a game there. Then he transferred back to Notre Dame for his last two years in college. Drafted in 1979 by Cleveland in the third round—the 65th pick—Laimbeer didn't make the Cavs, so he went to Italy, where he played 29 games for a team called Brescia in the Italian League.

In 1980–81, he came to Cleveland's rookie camp. "Everybody thought there was no way he'd be in the league," notes Detroit coach Chuck Daly. "Bill would have probably said the same thing. Nobody could project what would happen to him."

Surprisingly, Laimbeer made the Cleveland team, but his image was that of a guy who couldn't run, couldn't jump, whose shooting ability was just adequate. Then, on February 16, 1982, he was traded to Detroit along with Kenny Carr for Phil Hubbard, Paul Mokeski, and a first- and second-round draft choice in 1982. The trade proved to be just the break Laimbeer needed. He became Cinderfella on the Pistons. Since that time he's been among the leading rebounders in the NBA, and he led the league in 1986. Four times he's made the All Star team. Not bad for a 65th pick who almost everyone wrote off.

James Lee Donaldson III was born on August 16, 1957, in Heachham, England. He's one of several guys in the NBA who were born in foreign countries. But what makes Donaldson a little different from the rest of the bunch is that I've picked him for my "All Cinderfella" team.

Donaldson played his college ball at Washington State University and was drafted by Seattle in the fourth round—the 79th pick in 1979. After almost a decade in the NBA with Seattle, then San Diego, then the L.A. Clippers, Donaldson has finally found a home with the Dallas Mavericks. One of the league's best rebounders, the 7'2" center says, "Guys like me and Laimbeer have proven that you don't have to be the most graceful guys in the world to succeed if you have the right work ethic."

Kevin Duckworth was voted the "NBA Most Improved Player" for 1987–88—and he earned it. Although he had a pretty good collegiate career at Eastern Illinois University, the seven-foot, 280-pound Duckworth looked like he was going nowhere for a while in the pros. San Antonio picked him in the second round—the 33rd pick overall—in the 1986 draft. But he didn't fit in with the Spurs and saw little playing time.

On December 18, 1986, Duckworth was traded to Portland for Walter Berry, and there were a lot of people who thought San Antonio pulled a fast one.

Duckworth averaged less than 6 points and 4 rebounds a game in 1986–87, but the next year he really came on, boosting his scoring average to 15.8 a game and his rebounds to 7.4 a game. The year after that he upped both totals. "I'm the type of person," Duckworth said, "that if you tell me I can't do something, I'm going to do it. Deep inside I knew I could do it, and that I would work hard to achieve it."

His full name is Anthony Jerome Webb, but that's too big a moniker for a little guy like that. Spud Webb suits him just fine.

Spud is one of the best Cinderfella stories ever. Drafted in the 4th round (the 87th pick by Detroit in 1985), put on waivers, and then picked up by Atlanta as a free agent, he's turned out to be pound for pound one of the best players in the NBA because of all the things he can do.

They have Spud listed at 5'7" and 135 pounds; I think he's smaller and lighter than that. But he's a strong little guy. Spud is the kind of player others don't like to defend against; guys don't even like playing against him. He has great speed, so if a defender plays up on him,

Spud can blow right by the guy. He also has a pretty good outside shot, and when he has that working, it's impossible to defend against him.

It's to Atlanta's credit that they not only took a chance with him but that they also developed him. He played his college ball at Midland and North Carolina State, but didn't average many points. I guess Atlanta coach Mike Fratello wanted a guy around who was about his size.

Spud is the kind of player I would have liked to coach. He doesn't say much but he does a lot of things on the floor. He's another coach out there, and he does whatever you tell him to do or try. Spud seldom goes off on his own or gets out of control, and he's very team oriented. Every time I've seen him in action, I've noticed he's always thinking pass first.

One of the great parts of Spud's game is his ability to penetrate. When he does that he's always thinking about making the pass. He's also so quick and agile that he hardly ever gets nailed inside and when he does, he's tough enough to shrug it off.

Spud is very unusual because of his size, but he's also a marvelous player, a joy to watch out there. In my day no one would want to go near him because of his speed. He's steady, not fancy, even though he did show how fancy and flashy he could be when he won the Slam Dunk competition a few years ago.

A great crowd pleaser at home and on the road, Spud at his size has got to be at least four times as good as anyone else. And don't bet he isn't.

Mike Riordan was perhaps the most successful "Cinderfella" that I ever coached. He came out of nowhere to become a pretty good player.

The 1967 draft lasted ten rounds, and Mike was still available after all the picking was done. We made him a supplementary pick for the Knicks and no one was ever sorry about it. At Providence College Mike had played in the shadow of Jimmy Walker, who was then one of the best players in the country. That was one reason that Mike went so low in the draft. He was also a little rough around the edges, but that roughness helped him to survive in the NBA.

A tough, New York Irish kid, Mike was very strong. He worked very hard and had the ability to ignore pain. I saw immediately that he was prepared to do whatever was needed to stay in the league.

Always working out as hard as he could, always playing one-on-one basketball in practice with anyone he could find, Mike would even work out before games, then take a shower and then be ready to go out there and play. He was always ready physically and mentally to play.

At that time in the NBA you were able to give up one point to try and get two by fouling a guy and then getting possession of the ball after he took a foul shot. My scheme was to use Mike as a designated foul-giver. I would put him into the game just to give a foul and then get him back on the bench. It was a tactic I used to keep the starting guards out of foul trouble. Most guys might have resented doing what Mike did, might have thought that to go into a game just to give a foul was demeaning to them. But Mike understood that was his role on the team at the start, and he gave the foul gladly just to survive. He was real good at it. Guys couldn't get away from him. Mike went out there on the court and nailed them.

Mike played for the Knicks for four years. I still can see him standing or sitting at a counter in a fast-food restaurant eating a hot dog or a sandwich and reading a

newspaper. He was a typical New York guy. Year after
year, he became a better player for us and a favorite of
the fans. His shooting developed and his defense improved. It got to the point that his all-around value was
recognized by other teams even though he was mainly a
backup to Dick Barnett and Walt Frazier.

On November 10, 1971, I swung a trade with Baltimore that brought Earl Monroe to the Knicks. The price
was Dave Stallworth, Mike Riordan, and some cash. I
hated to see a guy like him go, but to get a player of Earl
Monroe's ability, we had to give up quality.

With Baltimore from 1971–76 Mike had his most
productive years. In the 1973–74 season, for example,
Mike played almost 40 minutes a game and averaged
almost 16 points a game. He became a real tough two-
way player.

Those years that Mike was on the Bullets usually saw
him matched up against Bill Bradley when we played
them. It was a funny scene because when they were teammates on the Knicks they spent many hours playing one-
on-one against each other in an empty gym after all the
other players had been long gone. A ninety-minute workout was never enough for either of them.

Mike Riordan, a tough Irish kid from the streets of
New York City, lasted a decade in the NBA and had some
really memorable moments. It was a tribute to his work
ethic that a guy like that, a supplementary pick, outlasted
many who were picked before him. Others picked out of
that same 1971 draft never became as successful as Mike
because they didn't have his work habits, his guts, or his
intelligence.

He was born Paul Keen Mokeski on January 3, 1957,
in Spokane, Washington, and he was grown up to be a

seven-foot, 255-pounder who doesn't look much like a basketball player. Drafted by Houston as the forty-second pick in 1979, Mokeski was traded to Detroit in 1980. Two years later, the Pistons traded him to Cleveland. The Cavaliers waived him, and he was signed by Milwaukee as a free agent. Now he's with Golden State, and into his second decade in the NBA. Not the swiftest guy around, not an especially good shooter, not one of your better athletes, he seems to be huffin' and puffin' out there on the basketball court. Yet he's made a career for himself in the NBA. I tip my hat to the big guy and have no hesitation in giving him a spot on my Cinderfella team.

9

The Franchise Players

eople are always asking me to name my personal All-time All Star team. When you've been around as long as I have, I guess they expect you to be some kind of expert. Well, I've probably seen as many basketball games as anyone that ever lived, and I've seen many great players, some really exciting players. But if I named an All Star team I'm sure I'd leave some guys out. So I'm not going to go out on that limb. (My last editor always said I was cagey.) But what I will do is go out on another limb—by giving you a rundown on who I think are the greatest franchise players ever.

To me, a franchise player is one who had or has an impact on the game, his team, the players he's given to work with, the fans. To me, franchise players are more than all stars. They're meal tickets.

A franchise player wants the ball when the game is on the line. He never blinks. When it's crunch time, he leads by example by demanding the ball. It's really a cliché to say that a player wants the ball in the clutch. Lots of players want it then. But the true franchise player not only wants the ball, not only is willing to get the ball, not only thinks he can do whatever has to be done when the game is on the line—he does it.

A franchise player makes the guys around him better. Teams double team and sometimes triple team franchise players. Game plans are set up around ways of stopping them. But a true franchise player gets around all of that and even makes the fringe players on his team better. He dishes off the ball to them, creating conditions that leave the fringe players open for easy shots, garbage baskets, fast-break opportunities. So just by being there and doing his thing, the franchise player makes the guys on his team play better, work harder. It's the old story: leading by example.

With the addition of a franchise player, the whole makeup of a team changes. The team may not automatically win a championship, but it does become a winner.

A franchise player has also got to be durable. He's got to be out there for forty minutes. He sits down only when the game is over one way or another.

Knowledge of the game, court savvy, intelligence—these are other qualities of a franchise player. They know the score in more ways than one. We'll be getting to my list in a few more paragraphs, but it's interesting to note that all the franchise players I picked have been coaches or executives or could have been or could be easily placed in leadership positions on teams. A couple on the list never took the opportunity. But that was not because they couldn't do the job—they just didn't want the aggravation.

MIKAN

George Mikan is the guy I consider to be the first franchise player in professional basketball history. At 6'10" and a burly 255 pounds, he was the most dominant force of his era. Wearing his glasses, taking his hook shots, passing the ball, playing defense—he was like Superman out there on the court.

George Lawrence Mikan Jr. was born on June 18, 1924, in Joliet, Illinois. He played his college basketball at DePaul University and became a national hero. He scored 53 points against Rhode Island State at Madison Square Garden in 1945. That year and the following year he led the nation in scoring.

In 1946, both the Basketball Association of America and the National Basketball League, the league I played in with the Rochester Royals, wanted to sign Mikan. Mikan made it clear that he wanted to play with a team in Chicago to be near his home. The Chicago Gears of the NBL offered him $12,500 for his first year; the other Chicago team in the BAA couldn't come up with the money to match the offer, and that's how Mikan came into my league.

A big strong guy with size and agility, a tough guy, Mikan could hurt you out there on the basketball court. In those days he'd scare you to death. There was nobody like him, nobody close to him. There were guys his size but not with his talent. He had that great hook shot, and he was so tough in the clutch. If you needed a basket and got it down low to him, he'd take care of things.

Mikan played in 25 games for Chicago in the NBL and averaged 16.5 points a game. But after his first season, the Chicago Gears folded. At a special National Basketball League meeting George Mikan was awarded to the Minneapolis Lakers.

That "awarding" changed the course of history in basketball in many ways. If not for that award my Rochester team would've been the greatest basketball team of that era. As it turned out, George Mikan made Minneapolis into basketball's first dynasty team. In that way he was a franchise unto himself. With Mikan on hand, Minneapolis won five championships in six seasons. He won three scoring titles, finished second twice, and third once. And he was a hell of a drawing card— probably the first great drawing card in basketball history. In New York City, when Minneapolis came to town, the marquee outside Madison Square Garden advertised: "TONITE—GEORGE MIKAN VS. KNICKS."

Philadelphia owner Eddie Gottlieb once offered his entire team (except for Paul Arizin, who was in the Marines at the time) in trade for Mikan. If Eddie had gotten the Marines to agree, he probably would have thrown Arizin into the deal, too.

Les Harrison, the owner-coach of my Rochester team, knew what we had to contend with and tried his best to do something about it. In 1947, Les spent $25,000 to acquire Arnie Risen from Indianapolis to counter Mikan. That was a lot of money back then. Risen had talent; Mikan had talent and heft and height. Arnie was overmatched.

Then Les brought in for a look see a 7'8" high school player named Max Palmer. The kid had heft and height, but not too much talent. He could hardly walk, and his coach had to hand him the ball to set him up for putting it into the basket. Max Palmer stayed with us for a short while before he went back to Iowa. One of my last memories of him was his sitting near our bench before we played a game against Minneapolis.

Mikan came over to the kid who respectfully stood up and looked down at George.

"There ought to be a law against these big jerks," George snapped. "They should bar these freaks from the game or do something to cut them down to size."

"Yeah, George." I couldn't resist it. "And they should start with you."

They actually did start with George. In 1951–52, the foul lanes were widened from six to twelve feet, and the rule was put in making it illegal for any player on offense to stay in the lane for more than three seconds. Those rules were definitely created just to cut George down to size. They didn't do too much. Although George's scoring average dropped from 28.4 to 23.8 points a game that '51–52 season, he killed my Rochester team with a 61-point game and led Minneapolis to another league championship.

Once my Rochester team played an experimental game against the Lakers. The basket was raised to a height of 12 feet to try to take away Mikan's edge. Raising the basket hurt us more than it hurt George. He still got his points. All we got were sore necks from straining to look up at the raised basket.

George Mikan would have been something to look up to in any era. On the basketball court he was a mean, tough guy. But he also had a sense of humor. Once I had the misfortune of jumping for a rebound against him— all he had was a 12-inch advantage and 70 or so pounds on me. I knew George would win the tip, but I didn't think he'd score a basket on it—and that's exactly what happened.

"That's the way to do it, George," I smiled. "You big schmuck. You have all the luck."

George smiled. His knowledge of Yiddish was more than limited—it was nil.

A few weeks later we played the Lakers again and George was not smiling. He came plodding over to me with a look in his eyes that could have pierced steel.

"I found out what the word 'schmuck' means, Red. You're gonna get it from me." He was a little bit more than agitated, and I wondered what translation of the word 'schmuck' had been given to him.

But I didn't wonder too long. I got my legs moving and got the hell out of his way. Fortunately, George was just kidding around. He could have killed me if he wanted to.

Speaking of killing, George Mikan, Number 99, was one of the toughest characters in the game, a guy who gave out a lot of punishment and also received his share.

He started off losing four teeth in his first game as a pro. Broken fingers and broken feet were part of the price he paid for the physical game he played. Some of his scars and bruises were nothing, though, compared to what he did to the opposition. One time when a couple of guys complained about how rough George's play was, he yanked off his jersey.

"What do you think these things are, birthmarks?" he snapped. His upper torso was a mass of welts and scratches. George once told me that he had counted 166 stitches that were sewed on him during his career to seal up the rips and tears put on his body by opposition players scratching and clawing at him.

I wound up my playing career as a member of the Milwaukee Hawks. We had scheduled about nine days in a row of playing exhibition games against the Lakers through the Midwest. It was hot as hell, and we traveled in the same bus with them. They beat the hell out of us every night, and then we had to get in the bus after the game and listen to those guys chirp about how good they were and how lousy we were. Those are memories of playing against George Mikan that I don't recall fondly.

I often read articles by guys who probably never saw George play. Despite the fact that he was voted "The Greatest Basketball Player of the First Half Century" by guys who saw him play, some of the new kids on the block have doubts about whether George could play in the NBA today. I have no doubts. George could not only play today, not only be a superstar, he'd be a franchise player.

Out of the pivot, he was probably the best passer I ever saw. If you covered him normally, he was an unstoppable scorer. If you double or triple teamed him, he would kill you with his passing. We weren't supposed to play zones, but we used to zone on him without the ball. Today you can't double team a man if he doesn't have the ball. No matter what teams did George still managed to get his points.

In an era when averaging 20 points a game was a big deal, Mikan flirted with a 30-points-a-game average. In 1948–49, only three players averaged 20 points a game; Big George averaged 28.3. A year later just two guys averaged 20 a game and Mikan was at 27.4. And the next year when he averaged 28.4 a game, only three guys averaged 20 or more a game.

Some interesting trivia associated with George is that his brother Ed was an NBA forward-center, and George's son Larry played as a forward for a year in the

NBA. George also was the American Basketball Association's commissioner during the 1968–69 season, when
they were looking for a name to give them some identity.

The one sad thing about Mikan's career was that it
was relatively short. He played just seven full seasons,
leading his teams to championships every one of those
seasons except one. Injuries and a desire to get on with a
law practice made him get out. In 1955–56, as a favor to
the Minneapolis owners, he staged a comeback. With
the 24-second clock, and his age and physical condition
against him, it was no longer his game. He played in
37 games and averaged just 10.5 points a game, and
finally called it quits for keeps. It was sad to see an all-
time great like George Mikan try to come back when his
time was past.

I prefer to remember him wheeling and dealing
in his prime—the glint coming off his big glasses, his left
elbow out there, the ball in his big hands, hooking another in for two points. George Lawrence Mikan Jr. was a
piece of work and a true franchise player.

RUSSELL

I sometimes wonder what it would have been like if I had
been given the opportunity to coach Bill Russell. Not
too many people probably remember, but I almost had
the chance. Back in 1956 I was coaching the St. Louis
Hawks. Russell was finishing up at the University of San
Francisco where he became only one of seven players in
NCAA history to average over 20 points and 20 rebounds a game during his career.

We drafted him for the Hawks and then Ben
Kerner, the Hawks owner, traded him to the Celtics
for Ed Macauley and Cliff Hagan. That all happened

because Ben Kerner knew he just didn't have enough money to sign Russell. The Hawks got two excellent players who helped them win five straight Western Division titles. But the Boston Celtics wound up with one of the greatest players of all time, a guy who totally turned around their franchise. With him there the Celtics won 11 NBA titles in 13 years, including eight in a row. He was the ultimate franchise player. Right off the bat in his rookie season he led the Celtics to their first NBA championship.

"Pride has always been very important to me," Russell said. "I love to win. It's the one thing that stayed with me right from the beginning." Right from the beginning everyone realized Russell's pride and the impact he would have as a franchise player.

Bob Cousy made the point and made it well: "Bill Russell meant everything to the Celtics. We didn't win a championship until we got him. We lost it when he was injured in 1958. We won it back when he was sound again in 1959. This was a team that had always been able to shoot. But when your defense is predicated on the fast break and you can't get the rebound—you haven't got a fast break."

Bill Russell set a pattern for the way the Celtics played, a pattern for team basketball, for defensive basketball, for pleasing basketball—at least for the Celtics and their fans. And that pattern to a degree still exists today on the Celtics.

My teams played against him and I spent many, many hours thinking up ways to cope with what he could do. The challenge he posed was intimidation. Russell would make players pull up or change their shot going to the basket. He wasn't bulky, but he was very strong and had those great reflexes.

With Russell there intimidating, the Celtics were able to run and were able to cheat on a lot of things because they knew he was back there if anything happened. If an offensive player thought he was free—well, he wasn't, not with Russell around. Bill had such great timing and reflexes as a shot blocker. When he blocked a shot he didn't just swat the ball into the seventeenth row. He'd block it to a teammate, and that's how the Celtics would get their fast break started—off his block. Then they would take off, knowing he would either get the rebound or block the shot. If they didn't have any good shots on the break, they still had Russell as a scoring option. He could put the ball in the hoop. People don't realize that he had a lifetime scoring average of 15.1, and most years he did a little better than that.

From 1957 to 1967 Russell played more minutes than any other Celtic and had the most rebounds. He was a workhorse, a guy who always seemed to dig down deeper to get that extra spark. He loved to play defense. Out of all the players I've seen through the years I have to rank Bill Russell as probably the most intelligent defensive player. He had anticipation, timing, a feel for the ball, and the knowledge of how to convert a defensive play on his part into a score for his team.

Even the challenge of Wilt Chamberlain didn't slow him down. When Wilt came into the league in 1959–60, many said that would be the end of Russell's run. Five inches taller than Russell and much bulkier, Wilt was a scoring machine.

"If I scored 40 points a game," Russell answered some critics, "then the other parts of my game would be suffering. I'd rather be what I am for a first-place team than a hot scorer for a third-place team . . . if Chamberlain is better than me," Russell continued, "then he's got to go out and show me. Every game. I'm never convinced."

Throughout most of the 1960s, wherever Chamberlain and Russell were matched up head to head, there was always a big crowd on hand and lots of debate about the abilities of two of the greatest franchise players of all time. Wilt was called a loser because his teams didn't win a championship, and Bill was called a winner because the Celtics were so dominant. But that was over-stating the case. Chamberlain's Philadelphia team was capable, but Russell was surrounded by a great supporting cast on the Celtics. And he was the first to admit it.

"I'm surrounded by a great collection of players," Russell said. "I may bring out the best in them, but they bring out the best in me. Can I perform the same function with another team?"

Chamberlain always tried to take all the controversy in his stride. It must have bothered him that Russell got the better of it in the press. "It's a vicious, real feud on the floor," he once said. "It's a pretend feud when we're together after the game. And when Russell gets named to the All Star team and I get left off—what am I supposed to do? Run screaming into the night?"

Their rivalry even showed up in salary negotiations. In 1965–66, Chamberlain signed a contract for the then record price of $100,000. "If Wilt is worth $100,000," Russell told Red Auerbach, "then I'm worth more." The Celtics signed Russell to a contract for $100,001—one dollar more than Chamberlain got. And I'm sure that was probably the most satisfying dollar Bill Russell ever earned.

On April 18, 1966, Bill Russell became the first black man to coach a team in any professional league. With the retirement of Red Auerbach, Russell took over as player-coach of the aging Celtics. He was still the franchise, and he knew it. "The best player I've got is me," he said, "so I'm the one I have to bear down the most on."

Russell grabbed 1,700 rebounds and averaged more than 13 points a game in his rookie season as a player-coach, but the Celtics finished second in the Eastern Division and were eliminated in the playoffs by the 76ers. A lot of people wrote off Russell and the Celtics after that season—too old, he can't coach, the end of an era. Those were some of the nicer lines people tossed about.

All Russell did after that was to lead the Celtics to two straight NBA titles. He always liked a challenge. In 1967–68, the Celtics won their 10th title in 12 years by defeating the Lakers in six games. Russell as a player and as a coach led the way.

In the 1968–69 season, the aging Celtics finished in fourth place during the regular season. Russell was thirty-five years old. But he kept reminding everybody that he was still Bill Russell. The Celtics got by Philadelphia and then the Knicks in the playoffs and were matched against the Lakers in the championship finals. L.A. had added Chamberlain to go along with greats Jerry West and Elgin Baylor. It seemed to many that it was no contest.

The teams split the first six games, which set up the seventh game on Monday, May 5, 1969, before a national TV audience and a packed house at the L.A. Forum. Boston held on to pull out a 108-106 win for its 11th NBA title in a game that was marred by controversy. Russell led the Celtics to victory while Chamberlain hobbled by a knee injury, took himself out of the game with about six minutes left to play. "Any injury short of a broken leg or a broken back isn't good enough," Russell later said. He was kind of rubbing salt into the wound that was his rivalry with Wilt.

But it was Jerry West who best summed up the Chamberlain-Russell rivalry. "I think Wilt Chamberlain is a better basketball player than Bill Russell," he said. "But for one game I'd rather have Russell. How can I reconcile that? You have to be an athlete to understand that."

And Russell made this point. "I never said Chamberlain didn't have talent, but basketball is a team game. I go by the number of championships. I play to bring out the best in my teammates. Are you going to tell me that he brought out the best in West and Baylor?"

Bill Russell retired after that 1968–69 season, saying, "I've lost my competitive urge." With a record 40,726 minutes played, a record 21,721 rebounds, a record 11 championship teams, a five-time MVP, and selected as the "Greatest Player in the History of the NBA" by the Professional Basketball Writers' Association of America in 1980—William Felton Russell was a franchise all unto himself.

PETTIT

Bob Pettit was the first franchise player I ever coached in the NBA. Yet when he first came into the league there were some doubts about him. Robert E. Lee Pettit couldn't even make his high school basketball team until his junior year. Although he averaged nearly 28 points a game and was a big star at Louisiana State University in his home town of Baton Rouge, that was a college without much of a basketball tradition. He was also a gentle guy at the start, and that was a rap against him. But he was a true southern gentleman and one of my all-time favorite players.

The first pro game he ever played was against the defending champion Minneapolis Lakers in a high school gymnasium in Wolf Point, Montana. The Lakers kicked his butt in the first half. They just manhandled him. I called him aside during halftime and asked if he enjoyed being a professional player.

"Yeah, Mr. Holzman," he said. "I like it just fine. I'm having a real good time."

All the time I coached Pettit I rarely ever yelled at him, but that night I bawled the crap out of him for his own good. "Well," I screamed at him, "you might not continue to enjoy it that much if you let the opposition wipe the floor with you the way the Lakers are doing tonight. When the second half starts, I want you to go back out there with some fire in you. Don't take any more crap. Get out there and hit the first guy you can. Show them all that you mean business."

The second half began and I knew that Pettit was looking to make contact with the smallest guy he could find. That was Slater Martin, 5'10", 165 pounds, small but tough. Pettit swung an elbow. Martin ducked his head. Pettit's elbow smashed into the chest of Vern Mikkelsen, one of the bruisers in the NBA back then.

"Excuse me, Mr. Mikkelsen," Bob said.

Pettit hadn't planned it that way, but he was able to send a message that he couldn't be intimidated—and the message got out all around the league.

Pettit was 6'9", 215 pounds, and mobile. I realized that he would fit in best as a power forward and moved him from the center position he was used to. I could see that he was not only a fine inside shooter, but also a great outside shooter. I taught him how to use his weight, how to block out under the boards, how to rebound off the offensive boards, how to go off a screen. He was a guy who practiced for hours and hours until he got it right. It took time teaching him to shoot facing the basket instead of with his back to it, but he became better and better as he developed confidence.

A very conservative type, Bob drove an old car and never put on the dog. At LSU he had referred to his coach as "Coach Harry." But he called me "Mr. Holzman."

I didn't like that too much. "Don't call me Mr. Holzman," I would always remind him.

"All right, Mr. Holzman, whatever you wish."

Pettit dropped the "Mr. Holzman" but could never bring himself to call me "Red." It was always "Coach William." That formal southern breeding was a tough thing for him to lick. I always called him "Schlim," meaning slim. And even though he was thin, he was a powerful athlete with a lot of stamina. His first season he played in 72 games and 2,659 minutes, a lot of minutes. He averaged 20.4 points and 13.8 rebounds a game and was voted Rookie of the Year.

In those days we sometimes played on neutral courts in preseason or even during regular-season games. Once we were in a place where the basketball floor had been put down on top of the hockey ice. The floor was slippery, just like a skating rink. Pettit went down once. Once was enough for me. I didn't allow him to play the rest of that game. He was the franchise right from the start—and I wasn't about to let the franchise get hurt.

Always prepared to play, always wanting to play, always asking questions and anxious to improve, Bob wasn't the fastest guy in the world but he could always get to where he had to go on the court. And when he got there he could shoot the ball. I've never seen a power forward who could shoot the ball as well as he could. Just how fine a shooter Bob Pettit was is seen in the fact that he was the first NBA player to score more than 20,000 points.

This was a guy who averaged 26.4 points a season, and even in his final season averaged 22.5. There were so many times that he passed up shots when he was double teamed. That's just one of the things that made Bob such an outstanding franchise player—his knowledge of the game and his unselfishness. Many other players lived off him. His being there on the court made them better players. His passing to them gave them easy baskets.

Offensive rebounding was another one of his strengths. Bob's stats in that area are outstanding— almost 13,000 in an 11-year career. A first-team All Star player every year but one. Bob won two MVP awards and three times was the Most Valuable Player in the All Star Game.

It was on April 12, 1958, during Bob's fourth season, that he probably had the most outstanding game of his career. It was the St. Louis Hawks against the Boston Celtics in the sixth and deciding game of the NBA Finals. Bob scored 50 points, including 19 of the last 21 scored by the Hawks, to give them their only NBA championship. That was how he could carry a team.

When Pettit's great career came to an end in 1965, there were the 125 stitches he had in his face during his career, the four broken bones in his back, the torn-up knee, the two scoring titles, the honors as a member of the NBA 25th and 35th Anniversary All-Time Teams . . . and plenty more. He had come to play, and anyone who ever saw Bob Pettit do his thing will never forget it.

Bob was another guy who left the game when he was on top.

ERVING

Julius Erving, better known to the basketball world as "Dr. J", was a two-way franchise player; he not only made his team better, but he was also one of the greatest showmen in the game's history.

His stats are stunning: picked to the NBA's 35th Anniversary All Star team, won an NBA championship with the Philadelphia 76ers in 1983 and two more with the Nets in the American Basketball Association in 1974 and 1976, played in 11 straight NBA All Star Games and won two MVP awards doing that, named to the NBA first-team All Star team five times, selected twice as the ABA Most Valuable Player and once as NBA MVP. . . . the list goes on and on.

Nowadays there's a big fuss made over power moves, slam dunks, spins, picks in the air, all the razzle dazzle that the players in the NBA use to show off their game. But the man born as Julius Winfield Erving in Roosevelt, New York, on February 22, 1950, was doing those things all by himself before they were in vogue.

I remember coaching the Knicks against him and his team, the New Jersey Nets, in a home-and-home exhibition series at the Garden and then the Nassau Coliseum in October of 1973. It was the first time the two teams had ever played each other. My Knicks at the time were the NBA champions, a team with such defensive talents as Walt Frazier, Dave DeBusschere, and others. We were a team geared to helping out on defense.

But Dr. J did his thing anyway. In those two games we played him and his Nets, the American Basketball

Association champions, Julius did his streaking layups, reverse dunks, sky dunks, spin moves . . . we keyed on him, but the guy was a one-man show.

Dave DeBusschere, who prided himself on his defense, told me: "You don't want Erving to get the ball off the break. If he gets the ball then you're in trouble. His speed, jumping ability, body control in the air, and ball control on the floor make him nearly impossible to stop. If he gets the ball on the run in the open field . . . well . . . you can almost forget it."

Dr. J seemed to have never forgotten anything he had done on a basketball court. When people asked him how he was able to do the things he did, he explained: "Nothing is premeditated. Ninety percent of the things I do, I've done before, either in a regular game or in a playground setting. The other one percent—well, I even surprise myself."

Erving grew up on Roosevelt, Long Island, playing basketball. It was when he was in high school that he got his nickname, but it was not well-known then.

"A friend in high school," Erving said, "told me he was going to be a professor, so I told him I was going to be a doctor." We started calling each other 'professor' and 'doctor.' Then in 1972 when I was playing ball in the Rucker League in New York City, it seemed everybody had a nickname for me. They called me 'Houdini' and 'the Black Moses' and other colorful names. I told them if they were going to call me anything, call me 'Doctor.' That became my nickname."

A star at the University of Massachusetts, Erving left college after his junior year. "I've done everthing I can playing where I am," he said. "I can always go back to college but what I want to do right now is make money." He made money.

There was a rule back then that neither the ABA or the NBA could sign a college player whose class had not graduated. But the Virginia Squires of the ABA in 1971 challenged the rule and went out on a limb and signed Erving for a bundle of cash. He had two great years with that team.

And then he got even better when he was traded to the New York Nets in 1973. He was not just a franchise player for the Nets—he became a franchise player for the ABA. Guys in the National Basketball Association were household names back then. But Dr. J gave the NBA stars a run for their money. His dazzling ways on the court, his personality off the court, his scoring outbursts—all of these helped give the American Basketball Association an identity all its own.

In four years with the Virginia Squires and the New York Nets, Erving averaged 28.7 points a game, leading the ABA in scoring each year. He was always among the leaders in steals, blocked shots, even rebounds. His versatility was unbelievable. Dr. J could play guard, forward. He probably could've even played center pretty well—except that at 6'7", even though he had the great leaping ability, he didn't have the height.

I was coaching the Knicks during Julius' glory years in the NBA, and I had enough on my mind getting our team into the playoffs. But I read the newspaper accounts of what he was doing, and sometimes buddies would come along and tell me about some of his heroics on the court.

Some of his games were mind-boggling:

In his rookie season with Virginia, Julius scored 53 points in a game against the Nets. There was 1:14 to go, and he was 14 points short of the ABA record. Al Bianchi, until recently the now Knicks' general manager and then the coach of Virginia, was asked if he was going to let Julius shoot for the all-time record.

"That's eleven more points in 74 seconds?" snapped Al. "Julius is great, but he's not Superman."

In a game against the Kentucky Colonels all he did in 45 minutes was to hit 12 of 24 field-goal attempts, take 18 foul shots and make 18 foul shots, and dish the ball off for ten assists.

The great success of Julius Erving was probably one of the reasons that the NBA and the ABA merged. Dr. J was such a draw, such a showman—there were very few guys in the NBA of his stature at that time. It was a little bit like echoes of George Mikan coming into the NBA.

On October 20, 1976, Erving was sold by the Nets to the Philadelphia 76ers for three million dollars. He had asked the Nets to renegotiate his contract according to the standards for superstars in the NBA. The Nets didn't have the money so they sold him. I drooled at the thought of getting Dr. J on the Knicks. I would have loved to have coached him and had his firepower on our side. But Mike Burke, then President of the Knicks, told me that the Nets wanted more money from us than any other team—four million was the asking price for Julius. At that time Burke thought that was steep even for a franchise player of his worth. In the long run, of course, it would have been a bargain.

His presence on the 76ers gave the Philadelphia franchise an identity it hadn't had in years. And Dr. J picked up as a player and as a leader right where he had left off in the ABA. Unfortunately, he wound up with a team in the same division as Boston. Although the Erving 76ers made the playoffs each year he was on the team, they always wound up second fiddle to the Celtics.

Whenever my Knicks played against him and the 76ers, I was always concerned about his agility and his ability to intercept passes and break away for quick baskets.

I have one unhappy memory of his breaking away that I'll never forget. It was the last game of the 1979–80 season—Philadelphia versus New York. Micheal Ray Richardson threw an inbounds pass right into the hands of Julius Erving. The doctor took off with the gift ball. He dribbled down the length of the court, went up and put both knees into the chest of Toby Knight, and dunked the ball. That shot went in right at the buzzer and won it for them. It also kept us out of the playoffs. I was more than a little upset. They never called the foul. But that's what reputation means in basketball; that's what happens with franchise players. They make their breaks and they sometimes get the breaks.

On April 17, 1987, Erving joined Kareem Abdul-Jabbar and Wilt Chamberlain as the only players to score 30,000 points in their pro careers. Dr. J scored 38 points for Philadelphia in the final regular-season home game of his career. It was quite a way for him to go out.

To his credit, Julius Erving went out when he was still productive. In his 16th and final professional basketball season, he averaged almost 17 points a game and over 18 in the playoffs, and he scored 22 in the All Star game. He could have still played a few more years, hanging on, but that's the kind of guy he was—a class individual who knew when he had enough.

There have been all kinds of guys that have played pro basketball. Julius Erving was a special talent. He gave the pro game an identity. Articulate, gentlemanly, a player everybody felt nothing but respect for, he was one of a kind. Not only was he a great franchise player, he's a sure Hall of Famer.

SCHAYES

One of my most vivid memories of Dolph Schayes is of an encounter I had with him when I was a scout for the Knicks. He was in his prime then as a star for Syracuse and had just finished up his practice and had broken a good sweat. I was all spiffy, at least that's what people told me, in my Brooks Brothers suit.

"Hey, Dolph," I called out, "let's shoot five for five from the circle to see who's better. I won't even take my jacket off."

"You gotta be kidding, Red. You're not in shape."

"You are—so let's give it a try, just for fun."

Dolph hit four out of five shots. I had my opening, and I made the most of it. I hit five out of five.

"Let's have a rematch, Red," Dolph insisted. A guy with an awful lot of pride in his shooting ability, he was a bit bothered that I had beaten him.

"No rematch, Dolph," I told him. "As long as we live, I'll be able to talk about what I did. You're one of the greatest shooters ever, and having beaten you today is something I want to have over you."

Dolph began to moan and complain. He wanted a rematch, but he never got one. Whenever we meet today, he still talks about that time and demands his rematch. He'll never get it.

But he does get my nomination as a franchise player.

Dolph Schayes is one of the guys who seems to get overlooked when people start talking about the best that ever played the game. He's in the Hall of Fame and is named to a lot of All-Time All Star teams, but somehow people don't make quite as big a deal about him as they should.

When he came out of NYU into the pros in 1948–49, there were some questions about his toughness, his durability. He was 6'8" and a thin 220.

The Knicks of the BAA drafted Dolph as did Tri-Cities of the National Basketball League. The Hawks realized they didn't have a chance to sign him so they transferred their rights to Dolph to the Syracuse Nats.

All along, Dolph wanted to play for the Knicks. He had been born and brought up in New York City, played high school ball at DeWitt Clinton, and would have been an incredible gate attraction with the Knicks. It was not to be because the BAA had a ceiling of $6,000 on first-year players; Syracuse offered $7,000 and Dolph signed with Syracuse. Some heat was directed against the Knicks and Ned Irish for not going for the extra thousand and signing Schayes. But it wasn't a case of the Knicks not going for the extra thousand. It was a case of their going by the rules. They honored the ceiling that had been set on rookies even though other teams did not.

Winding up with Syracuse proved to be a great thing for Schayes. He's admitted that himself. "Had I gone with New York," he said, "I might not have become the player I did. With Syracuse I had the chance to play regularly and improve myself. Playing with a team in the big city is not easy. The fans are not as patient as they are in the smaller one. I'm happy the way things worked out. I have no regrets."

At Syracuse, Schayes was also surrounded by veteran players like Fuzzy Levane and a smart coach in Al Cervi. Those guys had played "Eastern-style" ball all their lives; they believed in movement, team basketball, and passing the ball to the open man. They sort of looked out for him and made sure that he got the ball at the proper time. That helped his confidence and eased him from college into the pro game.

Howard Cann, Dolph's coach at NYU, also deserves credit for the proper training he gave. All the time Dolph was in college he played facing the basket, unlike someone like Bob Pettit who came into the pros playing with his back to the basket. Pettit had to make a big adjustment; Schayes did not, aside from learning the pro game. He was one of those players who turned out to be better in the pros than he had been in college.

Syracuse won only one NBA championship all the time Dolph was there, but you couldn't blame him for that. He was a franchise player, a guy who was a perfectionist, an athlete who always worked on improving his game. He averaged 16.8 points in his second pro season and six years later was at 20.4 a game. He averaged 24.9 two years after that.

A real student of shooting, Dolph practiced and repeated what he had practiced. That's lonely, tough work, a big price to pay. Pettit was like that, too. Larry Bird also shoots hundreds of shots in practice. Guys like Schayes, Pettit, and Bird do that practice shooting out of a desire to get better and better and also out of a love for the game.

They gave Schayes the nickname "The Rainbow Kid" because of the high arc he had on his shots from way outside. He once explained to me that he felt with more arc on the basketball he was increasing the angle of the ball's descent and making the target area bigger. Dolph explained that the basketball's circumference was nine inches smaller than that of the basket. That's why in shooting practice he put a circular lid with a smaller opening on the basket. He figured that by shooting at a smaller hoop in practice, it would be easier for him to hit his shots in a real game with a bigger hoop there. I don't know if I buy all those theories, but it worked for Dolph Schayes. He was one of the greatest shooters I have ever seen.

His foul shooting was also exceptional. Dolph shot almost 85% from the foul line—and that was for his entire career. He led Syracuse in foul-shooting percentage eleven straight years. Can you blame me if I never gave him a rematch?

From a historical perspective, I guess Dolph has to be considered one of the first big, mobile forwards. He was in constant motion all the time—inside, outside, baseline, and he averaged almost eleven rebounds a game for his career.

There was nothing one-dimensional about Schayes. He could beat you in so many ways. That was his great strength as a franchise player.

One of his special skills was in getting the three-point play. He had great range as a shooter and he'd wait with his outside shot. If a player came up on him, Dolph would put the ball on the floor and drive to the basket. He wouldn't go up for his shot until he had the defensive player out of position. Then he'd go up for his shot and draw the foul.

Dolph made the others on his team play better because other teams keyed on him. And when they did he could make the pass or free up others on his team for a shot. He was greatly responsible for the success of Syracuse.

They questioned Dolph's durability when he first came into pro ball; they didn't question it when he left. The guy was so consistent, so much into the work ethic that people took him for granted. In the 1959–60 season, he became the first NBA player to score more than 15,000 points in a career. He wound up with nearly 20,000. Rolling on like Ol' Man River, Dolph played sixteen years, and twelve of those years he was on the All Star team. He played in three decades—the '40s, '50s, and '60s. No one has really overlooked him, but had he played in New York City he would have received much more recognition. And if he were playing today, he'd be a leading three-point shooter and a two-million dollar-a-year ballplayer.

WEST

Another piece of trivia news that I thought you'd appreciate is the fact that Jerry West is the model for the silhouette of the player on the NBA logo. That's just one way he's been honored for all his accomplishments in basketball. A member of the Basketball Hall of Fame, named to the NBA 35th Anniversary All-Time team in 1980, Jerry West is one of the few guys I would have gone out of my way to pay to see play. He was something special in addition to being a great franchise player.

Jerome Alan West was born on May 28, 1938, in Cheylan, West Virginia. That's one of those towns that's so small it didn't even have its own post office. In his adolescent years, Jerry spent most of his time shooting around at a neighbor's house where there was a basket on the garage wall. He led his high school to the West Virginia state championship in his senior year.

At West Virginia University, Jerry averaged nearly 25 points a game for his four years as a varsity starter. In 1959, his West Virginia team lost the NCAA championship game to California by one point. Jerry did all he could—he was the leading scorer and MVP in the tournament.

Jerry West and Oscar Robertson formed a great one-two punch on the 1960 Olympic Basketball team that easily won a gold medal. Then, in the NBA draft, Robertson and West went one-two.

Ironically, if the draft rules in 1960 were the way they are today, the Knicks could have had West or Robertson. Cincinnati got Oscar as a territorial choice. The Lakers were able to pick West even though they finished third in their division in '59 and the Knicks finished fourth. That was because the Lakers had a record that overall was two games worse than the Knicks.

Never before in all the years of the draft had the second guy picked been of the quality of West. And yet some so-called experts had reservations about him becoming a big star in the NBA despite what he had accomplished at West Virginia. They said he was too small at 6'4", too skinny at 185 pounds, and too fragile and injury-prone (he had suffered a couple of broken noses in college and there would be more later on).

The Lakers moved from Minneapolis to Los Angeles in 1960–61, West's rookie year. In college Jerry had been a freelance operator, a guy who played up front and in the backcourt, a guy who accounted for most of West Virginia's scoring. With the Lakers it was a different situation. They had Elgin Baylor inside, so Jerry played outside. And it took him a little while to learn to handle the backcourt with all of its intricate offensive and defensive problems. He had a good rookie year, averaging 17.6 points a game, 16th in the league. But he was overshadowed by Robertson, who was third in scoring with over 30 points a game. Some of the guys who had expressed doubts about Jerry were starting to do a little talking.

I never had any doubts about him. Jerry West was just one of the greatest players ever to get out on the court. I never liked it or felt too comfortable when he was out there against my teams.

We played the Lakers in the 1970 NBA finals. That was a team with three-fifths of the league's first string All Star team: West, Baylor, and Chamberlain. We all knew it was going to be tough.

In the second game of the playoffs West scored 34 points; he was kind of unstoppable. In the third game, played in L.A., we had a two-point lead with three seconds left. A disgusted Wilt Chamberlain, sure his team had lost, just flipped the ball inbounds to Jerry West. He turned and heaved the ball. It was a desperation shot, a 55-foot shot, but incredibly, it went in. Chamberlain was halfway to the Laker locker room when the shot went in. They had to call him back on the floor.

All of us on the Knicks were stunned by what West had done. It was unnerving—a game that had seemed sewed up was going into overtime. But in no way were we going to lay down and quit.

Dick Barnett spoke for all the Knicks when he said, "Aw man, let's forget it." We did, and we beat the Lakers in OT and moved toward the first world championship in Knick history.

Throughout his entire career, West followed a pattern that had begun in his rookie season: when the game was on the line, when the stakes were the highest, Jerry West was there. All during his career he always averaged more points in post-season pressurized play than he did in the regular season.

They gave Jerry West the nickname "Mr. Clutch," and he certainly deserved it. He knew how to shoot.

He'd go up in the air, lean in, get the foul, and make the foul shots.

I would always kid him. "Jerry, if I got the breaks that you get when I was playing, I'd still be playing." Even a line like that didn't break his concentration.

Jerry had great concentration, control, and confidence in what he was doing, and he knew what he could do. He was able to set himself up, no matter who was guarding him, to get free for his shot.

If you fouled him at a crucial time in the game, he was like a cash register. Jerry never seemed to miss when a game was on the line. If he had an opening for a shot, it was automatic for him to score. West had an excellent jump shot and could hit it from any spot on the floor. Off his dribble he was a very skilled assist man. He would always manage to hit a free man on his team. Even in his final year as a player he averaged almost seven assists a game. In those days that was a lot for a shooting guard. And his offense sometimes obscured the fact that he was a hell of a defensive ballplayer.

In 1971–72, he was a big reason for the Lakers beating my Knicks in the Finals and finally winning an NBA championship. That season he helped L.A. win 33 in a row, and he was the MVP in the All Star Game and led the league in assists.

Like all franchise players, West had that killer instinct, and although he was a 6′4″ guard, he wasn't afraid to get in there under the boards and mix it up. Unfortunately, he paid a price for that determination— eight times in his career he had his nose broken. And he was out of action for other stretches of time because of injuries. But he never spared himself, never quit.

"I don't mind people depending on me," he used to

say. "Pressure makes me want to play harder. As the game goes on, the harder things are, the better I like it. The challenge seems to lift me up."

In his second season in the NBA he had a real challenge. Forced to take on the leadership and the scoring of the Lakers when Elgin Baylor suffered a serious knee injury that put him out of action for half the season, West finished fourth in the league in scoring at 30.8 points a game.

Jerry's number-one booster was his coach, Fred Schaus. "Few would be willing to work as hard as he has to improve," Schaus said. "I scouted him in high school and coached him four years in college and then in the pros. It's not just the plays he makes and the points he gets," Schaus said, "but it is the inspirational leadership he gives and the things he does when we need them the most that makes him mean so much to us. In all honesty, although I've had many great players, I have to say he is the greatest clutch player I've ever coached . . . or even seen, for that matter."

After his spectacular second season, West just kept improving each year. Twice in the next five seasons he averaged 31 points a game; twice he averaged 28 points a game. On January 17, 1962, against the New York Knicks in Los Angeles, he scored 63 points, the most ever recorded by an NBA guard to that point in time.

There was only one thing that could stop Jerry West—illness or injury. And sometimes not even that could stop him, merely slow him down. Once, he wore a mask to protect a broken nose, and he scored 38, 47, 42, 39, and 53 points in five successive games.

"I want to do well so much it makes me sick," West once said. "To me the hardest part of the game is sitting around waiting. I'm just awful to my wife and kids on game days, and I'm just glad when I can get the heck out of the house and into the arena."

The 1968–69 season was probably the time of Jerry West's greatest individual achievement and his biggest personal disappointment. He missed 21 regular-season games because of injuries but was in top form as usual for the playoffs.

Scoring 36, 36, 25, 36, 29, and 29 points, he led the Lakers past the San Francisco Warriors and then the Atlanta Hawks in five games in the Western Division finals. Then, for the sixth time in his career, West faced the Boston Celtics in the NBA Finals.

Scoring 53 and 41 points, West spearheaded the Lakers' wins in the first two games. But the Celtics won the next two in Boston. The Lakers won the fifth game, but West pulled a hamstring muscle and had to leave the game. West, physically sub-par in Game Six in Boston, still managed to score 26 points, but the Celtics won. The series returned to L.A. for the final game.

"I couldn't stay at home," West said. "I was too nervous. I couldn't wait to get to the arena that night. So I left the house early in the afternoon and drove around for a long time. Then I went down to Marina Del Rey. I just sat in my car looking at the boats and thinking. It was so peaceful and quiet there and I kept thinking, 'This is going to be some night.' I was getting all charged up for the game. I was sure we were going to win. It was some night, all right. It was a nightmare."

For three quarters that game was a nightmare for Jerry West and his Laker teammates. Going into the fourth quarter the Celtics led 91-76, and most had written L.A. off. Then West showed what a franchise player is made of. He took charge in that final period, leading a comeback that brought the Lakers back into the game.

In the end the drive fell two points short, and Boston knocked off its 11th title in 13 tries. But it wasn't Jerry's fault. He wound up with 42 points in the game for a total of 556 points and 135 assists for the playoffs. That was more than enough to get him named playoff MVP. It was rare for that kind of thing to happen to a guy who was on the losing team.

Laker coach Bill Van Breda Kolff said, "Maybe I took Jerry for granted all this time. Now I know he is the most complete ballplayer in the NBA today . . . and maybe of all time." I don't know if I would go out on that much of a limb. Bill coached Jerry. I never had the pleasure. But I do rank Jerry West as one of my top franchise players, one of the greatest players ever.

CHAMBERLAIN

They called him the "Dipper," but a lot of guys had other names for him, some of them unprintable. Whatever they called him, Wilt Chamberlain, at over seven feet tall and solidly built, was one of the strongest men in the world and one of the greatest offensive machines basketball has ever known.

In college at Kansas, Wilt averaged almost 30 points a game in two varsity seasons. Then he quit and signed on to play for the Harlem Globetrotters for a year.

Eddie Gottlieb of the Philadelphia Warriors had convinced the NBA to broaden its "territorial pick" rule, which only covered college players. He reasoned that it should also include high school. Chamberlain played his high school ball in Philadelphia, so Gottlieb drafted Wilt after his high school graduation and waited Wilt out for four years. He was worth the wait.

"Wilt Chamberlain is Babe Ruth all over again," was Eddie's motto. He certainly was. NBA attendance went up 23% during Wilt's rookie season. It seemed everyone wanted to see him in action. His impact on the NBA was something special.

Wilt's scoring was so prolific that people often forget that he was a hell of a player in other areas, too. In 1959–60, his first season in the NBA, he averaged 37.6 points a game and won the MVP and Rookie of the Year awards. The next season he set the all-time record for rebounds in a game, 55, against the Boston Celtics. Once he led the league in assists just because he made up his mind that was the thing he wanted to do.

I was there when Wilt played his first game against the Knicks at the Garden. He put on a show. Playing all but 15 seconds of the game, Wilt scored 43 points and grabbed 28 rebounds. My buddy Fuzzy Levane was the coach of the Knicks then and I felt a little sorry for him, knowing he would have to contend with Chamberlain a dozen more times that season.

"It ain't fair," Fuzzy complained after the game.

"Remember George Mikan, Fuzzy," I tried to comfort him.

"Yeah, Red, I remember Big George, but this guy ain't human."

Fuzzy's attitude was mild compared to what others thought of Chamberlain. They called him a monster and pointed out that what he did on the court was no big deal since he had a four- or five-inch height advantage over most centers he came up against.

"Like David and Goliath," Chamberlain answered his critics, "no one feels sorry for Goliath. He was killed by a smaller man. What they do is take a little bit away from the bigger man and give all the credit to the man who is inferior in height and weight, never realizing what the big man has to go through. It's human nature. No one roots for Goliath. I've been billed in so many places as the biggest player. If I was 6'8" or 6'9" and scoring 50 points a game it would be different. I would be regarded with more respect. I hear people say, 'All he has to do is dunk the ball.' I don't see how they can think that. I've got a lot of shots. They don't see that."

Scoring was Chamberlain's forte and scoring was what he got criticized for. A lot of people marveled at how he could put the ball in the hoop, but they also charged that he was a selfish player, a guy who hogged the ball, a one-dimensional player.

Wilt always had a lot to prove, a lot of detractors to take on. In 1968, when he led the league in assists, he became the first center in history to do so. Later in his career, Wilt decided he wanted to lead the league in field goal percentage, and simply shot a record 72.7% from the floor in 1972–73. He always had more than one dimension.

Wilt's night of nights took place on March 2, 1962, in Hershey, Pennsylvania. His Philadelphia Warrior team was matched against the New York Knicks. An exhibition game took place first between players from the Philadelphia Eagles and the Baltimore Colts, two pro football teams. Wilt was bigger and stronger than any of the guys on those teams.

In the first quarter Chamberlain popped in 23 points while the crowd chanted, "Give it to Wilt! Give it to Wilt!" The big guy was just warming up. He had an 18-point second quarter. Up to that game, the most points he had amassed in a contest was 78 points, but he had 69 points after the third quarter and seemed a cinch to break his record. However, no one expected him to do what he did. With 42 seconds left in the game, Wilt got the ball under the basket and stuffed it in with two hands—his 99th and 100th points. They had to hold up the game after he hit the century mark. Fans were all out on the floor rushing around trying to get to Wilt and congratulate him.

That was just an incredible performance. Although three Knicks scored over 30 in the game—Richie Guerin had 39, Willie Nauls put in 31, and Cleveland Buckner made 33—no one cared about that. It was Wilt's night. It hadn't been that long before when the first *team* scored 100 points. Chamberlain hit 36 of 63 field goal attempts and made 28 of 32 free-throw shots. With all the great scorers that have come along ever since, Wilt Chamberlain's record of 100 points in one game still stands as the all-time record.

After that game Wilt told anyone who would listen, "I wasn't even thinking of hitting 100 even though I had 59 at halftime. After putting in nine straight free throws, I was thinking about a foul-shooting record." That was always Wilt's fantasy—foul shots—and that was his only real weakness, making those foul shots.

My relationship with Wilt was cordial. In fact, I always spoke highly of him in the newspapers and especially praised his passing. That was because I hoped that he would read what I had said and then concentrate on passing instead of shooting.

They listed Wilt at 7'1", but I'm sure that he was taller than that. And he was a bull. He worked out mainly on his own with his own methods. He lifted a lot of weights and did a lot of running at the beach.

Chamberlain could have been outstanding in anything he did in sports—he was great in volleyball, boxing, track and field.

Part of his strength was his ability to come back from injuries. Wilt would get hurt and then come back so fast you couldn't believe it. An injury that would sideline another player for a month or more would lay up Wilt for a week.

I always told our centers not to touch him if he was under the basket going up in the act of shooting. Down under there was no way he'd ever miss scoring no matter how hard he was hit. He was just so powerful.

Offensively, there probably has never been a player that has been his equal. The season that he scored 100 points in one game, 1961–62, Wilt averaged 50.4 points per game. Today when Michael Jordan pours in 50 points in a game it's considered a big deal. What are you going to say about Chamberlain, who averaged 50 points a game for an entire *season?*

Kareem Abdul-Jabbar holds the record for consecutive games scoring in double figures at 787, but the rest of the big consecutive-game scoring numbers belong to Wilt. He scored 20 points or more in 126 straight games, 30 points or more 65 times, 40 points or more in a game 14 times, and 50 points or more 7 times. On March 10, 1963, playing for San Francisco, Chamberlain scored 70 points in a 163-148 loss to Syracuse. That was one of a half-dozen times in his career he scored 70 or more points in a game.

On the boards he was equally as dominant. In addition to the record for most rebounds in a game, he holds the record for most rebounds in a season, in a career, and highest rebounding average for both a season and a career.

   In 1968, the Philadelphia Warriors traded Wilt to
L.A. He was the final ingredient that made them a great
team. In the seventh game of the 1969–70 championship,
Wilt scored 21 points and grabbed 21 rebounds. But I
always joked that we held him to one for eleven from the
foul line. That was one of the factors that enabled my
Knicks to beat L.A. and give New York its first pro basketball championship ever. Wilt did not like to lose, but
he was a good sport about it. He even came into the
locker room after that game and shook my hand—gently.
That was always the way you wanted him to do that.
   In 1971–72, it was L.A.'s turn. That season, with
Chamberlain controlling things, the Lakers won 33
straight games, finished the regular season with a 69-13
record, and won their division by 18 games. My Knicks
met L.A. in the Finals. We didn't have Willis Reed. And
after the second game we didn't have Dave DeBusschere,
who got hurt. The Lakers beat us in five with Wilt charging things up. That was the first world championship for
L.A. in seven tries. Some people were finally starting to
forget the loser label they had pinned on Wilt. I didn't
forget after all the shouting had ended to go over and
shake his big hand—gently.
   To this day the man born as Wilton Norman Chamberlain on August 21, 1936, in Philadelphia is still a
controversial figure in basketball history. He had his
problems with coaches and the press. Sometimes it appeared that he shot too much; other times he wouldn't
put the ball up and concentrated totally on defense. He
was a force and a frenzy out there. He never fouled out
of a game and never could shoot foul shots. Both of those
items were raps against him. But you look at the record:
Hall of Fame 1978, MVP four times, All Star 10 times
. . . a 30.1 career scoring average, over 30,000 points

scored in his career, and almost 24,000 rebounds. Wilt Chamberlain was a franchise.

HAVLICEK

At Ohio State University, John Havlicek was the number-two man on a great basketball team that won the national championship when he was a sophomore and was runner-up the next two years. The number-one man on that team was center Jerry Lucas.

There were those who had their doubts as to whether John could make it in the NBA. Some thought he was too big at 6'5" for a guard position and too small for a forward. But to their credit, the Celtics saw Havlicek's potential and made him their number-one pick in the 1962 draft. It was the last pick in the first round—and another case of a guy who would become a great, great player after being overlooked by so many teams.

"I had seen him play only twice," Red Auerbach, then coaching Boston, recalled. "And he didn't look especially good. The reason I picked him was that he was a hard-nosed kid, well-coached, and a guy with good fundamentals."

As a rookie, Havlicek was a hit almost immediately. Moving without the ball was his forte and he moved, moved, moved—all the time. He averaged 14 points a game as a rookie playing less than 28 minutes a game. "I made a living off Bob Cousy's passes," the man they called "Hondo" said. His playing time increased to 32 minutes a game in his second season, and John averaged almost 20 points a game to lead all the Boston scorers.

Probably the greatest non-starter in basketball history, Havlicek said, "Whether I start or come off the bench makes no difference to me. It doesn't change anything. My game has always been to go as hard as I can as long as I can. I want my opponent to chase me. I want him to get tired and loaf maybe once or twice on defense. That's when I'll take advantage of him."

John Havlicek took advantage of a lot of guys in a lot of different ways. With him out there the game was never over. He'd always find something or some way to beat you. If it wasn't his defense, it was his scoring—outside and inside. He was an 81% career foul shooter, a guy who always wanted the ball in the clutch. But he didn't only want the ball—he'd shoot it and make the shot. In key games, must-win games, Hondo would come up with 35 or 40 points. He seemed to save his big scoring for those games.

All the time I coached Bill Bradley, he took it as a matter of honor, a compliment, that I asked him to guard Havlicek. Bill was as tough as they come, a really irritating player on defense. And although John was bigger and stronger than him, Bill played him very well. He would hound Havlicek all over the court, stick his hands all over him, do anything he could to throw John off his stride. Those Havlicek-Bradley matchups were classic battles. Both guys seemed to take their already intense game a notch higher when they played against each other.

A very pleasant guy, a very confident player, John Havlicek fit in perfectly in Boston with their scheme of team basketball. He has been quoted as saying that he was never a one-on-one player, but he could have been. However, John was at his best in a setup where he ran— where he could get into the open court. That was part of the Celtic approach as a team.

In that kind of context, Havlicek was a playmaker, a passer finding the open man, a guy who was out there creating things. He was a master at driving with the ball, spreading the defense, penetrating. I can still see him out there directing the Celtics, coming off a screen, and putting up his shots and getting his points.

John Havlicek was not only one of the great franchise players but probably the best sixth man of all time. An off guard and at the same time a small forward, he was the best shooting, jumping, rebounding, passing, ballhandling forward-guard of his era.

"I could start John if I had to," Red Auerbach said. "I don't start him because to me he's more valuable coming off the bench. He lights a fire under a team. He is the ideal swing man."

John not only was a guy who knew his role, he loved it. "Usually I come off the bench," he said, "to get the confidence of the team and get it running again—with a press, a steal, a long basket, anything."

Another set of qualities that made Havlicek such a great franchise player was his determination, endurance, and tenaciousness on defense. They estimated that he ran about three to five miles a game. It was like the Boston Marathon for those who had to come up against him. "His body is meant to go on forever," said Jerry West. "It's like he has a dozen legs."

The rap against Hondo when he first came into the NBA was turned around as his game developed. Now the party line became that John Havlicek was too big for most guards to handle and too quick for most forwards to cope with. It was no party line. It was the truth—he'd run most forwards ragged, and outmuscle most guards.

His court presence and awareness of what was going on around him was exceptional. John showcased these qualities game after game. And especially in playoff games.

In the final game of the 1965 Eastern championship, the Celtics had a 1-point lead with five seconds to go and Philadelphia in possession with enough time to score the winning basket. Waiting for Hal Greer to inbound the ball, John Havlicek sensed what Philadelphia planned to do: Hal Greer would give the ball to one of the forwards, circle to the corner for the return pass, and take a jump shot to win the game.

Guarding Chet Walker, John Havlicek began to count off the seconds. "One thousand and one . . . one thousand and two . . . one thousand and three . . ." When 3 seconds had elapsed and the ball had still not been inbounded, Havlicek turned in time to see Greer's looping pass. He leaped, got his fingertips on the ball and tapped it to Sam Jones. Time ran out on Philly.

The following year, also against Philadelphia, also in the final game of the Eastern playoffs, Havlicek missed six straight shots and Auerbach took him out of the game. Then Red put Hondo back. He missed two more shots, then hit seven straight to break the game open for Boston.

In the semifinals that year against Cincinnati, the Celtics had trailed in the five-game series, 2-1. Auerbach played Havlicek at forward and the Celtics won the next two games and the series. They went on to win the NBA championship in Auerbach's final year as coach.

By 1969–70, many of the Celtic stars, including Bill Russell, were gone. That forced the new coach, Tommy Heinsohn, to use Havlicek in a starting role. "I can't afford the luxury of having John come off the bench," Tommy said.

That decision showcased Hondo as a total player. He led Boston in scoring over the next five years, and in assists four of those five. He also hauled in about eight rebounds a game. That was one of the reasons most everyone thought of him as one of the best all-around players ever in the NBA. He strung together back-to-back seasons in 1970–71 and 1971–72 of playing 45 minutes a game, averaging 28.9 and 27.5 points a season.

A thirteen-time All Star, John led the Celtics to two world championships in the '70s. One of his great assets was his ability to play two positions—actually, not just play two positions but excel at them. There probably never was a swing man in the NBA like Havlicek—he was a first-team All Star at two different positions.

Havlicek was another one of those guys who quit the game when he was still very good. He came into the league when he was twenty-two years old and left it when he was thirty-five. In that span he played in 1,270 regular-season games and 172 playoff games. Even in his sixteenth and final season Havlicek still played in all 82 games and averaged 16.1 points playing almost 35 minutes a game. He wanted to leave when he was at the top of his game. That's the way I'll always remember John Havlicek—at the top.

BIRD

Larry Bird is another one of those players that I could have had the chance to coach if things had just fallen right. In the 1978 draft, when I was away from coaching, the New York Knicks selected Sugar Ray Richardson. They could have taken Larry Bird as a junior. And Larry would've joined the team the following season. But the Knicks wanted to get what they thought would be instant help and they went for Richardson. The Celtics picked Larry and waited a year. Bird made them into a great team. Of course it's all hindsight, but he was sure worth waiting for.

If the Knicks had shown that kind of patience Bird would have been on the team when I came back to coaching. I could have coached Bird and probably would still be there coaching him today.

I rate Larry Bird along with Jerry West as the best clutch player I have ever seen. Not only does Bird want the ball in the clutch, he knows what to do with it when he gets it. He's a player that is unselfish, a guy in the mold of the players on my championship teams. But he has more talent than any of those players had. However, when he has to be selfish for the good of the team he can be.

Larry has a great flair at hitting the open man. He plays hard all the time and he doesn't tolerate other guys on his team not playing the same way.

A first-team All Star each year he's been in the NBA, a three-time Most Valuable Player award winner, Larry Bird is an impact player. With him on the scene since the 1979–80 season, the Celtics have never failed to make the playoffs and they've won three championships. Larry Bird gets results and he makes his teams get results.

One of the things that has impressed me seeing him play is his great confidence in his ability. He will try shots that almost seem impossible to make—and he makes them. He'll also get into a shooting slump once in a while, but he'll keep putting the ball up. He knows he'll come out of that slump and the team defending against him will be burned.

That kind of attitude is what makes him such a great franchise player. It gives the players on his team confidence. He's proven to them over and over again what he can do on the court. They let Larry hold the ball, hog the ball, control a game flow. They know if he can't get off his shot, he'll get it to them.

Mental strength is another part of Bird's package. In his mind he doesn't see himself losing a game, and he doesn't allow his teammates to do so either. What I mean by this is that Bird can be down 20 points and still keep playing as if there's just a couple of points separating his Celtics from the other team. He brings Boston up to another level.

Look at the other players in the NBA and then look at Bird—so many of them are much better athletes. They can jump higher, run faster. At 6'9" and 220 pounds Larry has been called a blue-collar ballplayer; he's that but he's a special kind of blue-collar ballplayer. In his head he responds so much quicker; he's on his way to get to where he has to go while others think about getting there. He might not be the fastest athlete, but that quickness of mind puts him in his own zone, places him in his own league, makes him do something great offensively or defensively or both every game.

I've seen him have many great games, but the one that really stands out for me is what he did on May 22, 1988, in the seventh game of the playoffs against the Atlanta Hawks. It was one of the top individual performances in NBA playoff history as Bird took it upon himself in the fourth quarter to beat Atlanta. That exhibition demonstrated what Kevin McHale said about Larry: "He just won't let his team lose."

Coming off Kevin McHale and Robert Parish picks, Bird hit nine out of ten shots in that final quarter, scoring 20 points and winding up with 34 in the game. What he did gave the Celtics a 118-116 victory. The Larry Bird scoring show began with a 16-foot turnaround jumper. In the next six and a half minutes, he went on to score all but three of the Celtic baskets.

The one shot he took that really stands out for me was when he wound up in the middle of two guys like a slice of cheese in a sandwich. But he wouldn't be denied. Squeezing off a left-handed scoop shot that looked for sure as if it was going to be blocked, Bird followed the shot up with body English. The ball just popped up like a guided missile and went down. "It was like one of those crank toys," was Kevin McHale's description of the way Bird's shot looked. I agree that it wasn't pretty, but it got the job done.

That whole fourth-quarter exhibition under the most excruciating pressure shows why Bird is the ultimate kind of franchise player. The Hawks played him as well as anyone could expect. It wasn't as though he was scoring with no one around him. All the shots he was making were tough shots, always with somebody's hand in his face. And when he couldn't get his shot off because of a double or triple team, Larry was always looking to hit the open man.

"Every shot I took in the fourth quarter," Bird explained later, "I was concentrating on so as to make sure I got a good rotation on the ball. They were double-teaming me a lot in the first half, and I knew I was not going to score a lot of points against the double team. They didn't double on me much in the fourth period."

One of Larry's greatest strengths is his great overall knowledge of the game—his ability to see the entire court at all times, to see the ball at all times, and know where the ball is going or should go.

Bird gives the players on his team a good deal of confidence. He's the best player on the Celtics on and off the court in his practice habits and in his desire to play. He'd play 48 minutes if they'd let him.

A great shooter, passer, even a great rebounder, Bird is a complete player and a presence. And yet with all of this going for him, he still can't do what Bill Russell did, totally dominate the game. Only a center can do that.

There have been a lot of great players in the NBA in the last few years. Michael Jordan, Magic Johnson, and Larry Bird come to mind first. Who's the greatest? I'll stay out of that—you know I always avoid controversy. But I will say if I had to pick one guy out of the three to start a franchise—I'd consider myself lucky.

Just how much value Larry Bird is to the Celtics was seen in the 1988–89 season when he was out until March recuperating from foot surgery. Boston missed him badly. The team didn't look the same on the playing court, in its won and lost record (42-40) or in the standings—third in the Atlantic Division after five straight first-place finishes.

JOHNSON

Earvin "Magic" Johnson was born on August 14, 1959, in Lansing, Michigan. A star at Everett High School in Lansing, an All American at Michigan State—the Magic Man is destined to go down as one of the greatest players in NBA history. Yet there was a time when he wondered just how good he could be, when he doubted his abilities.

"I think it's mostly from where I cam from, a small town like Lansing," he said. "Nobody ever made it out of there," the 6'9" guard added. "And you always heard about the guys from New York, Detroit, Chicago, L.A., the big-city guys. I remember my biggest dream was to make All-City, get my picture in the newspaper. I never thought I'd do it. I always doubted myself, but I think that's what made me work harder to become the better player I have."

It was a coin flip on April 19, 1979, that brought Johnson to Los Angeles. The Chicago Bulls and the Lakers flipped for the first pick in the 1979 draft. The Bulls called heads. The coin came up tails and the Lakers got Magic Johnson.

Right from the start you could see the kind of player he was—and the kind of franchise player he was going to be. Magic has the ability to completely dominate smaller guards and play down low with the bigger players. In fact, Johnson is able to play forward and center at times. His combined height and ballhandling skill have allowed him to develop a skill for going "coast-to-coast"—grabbing a defensive rebound and dribbling downcourt for a layup on the other end. Pin-point passing ability, his knack of hitting the open man, often while looking in another direction—that's also part of his package.

In his rookie season, Magic showed the league his franchise-player value. He replaced Kareem Abdul-Jabbar, out with a sprained ankle, at center, and led the Lakers past Philadelphia in the sixth and final game of the 1980 Finals. He became the first rookie in NBA history to be named MVP of the Finals.

Magic's ability to make the players around him better even applied to veteran Kareem Abdul-Jabbar. "Before I got to the Lakers they all said that Kareem was stern and didn't smile," Magic said. "'You better watch out for him,' they told me. So when I came to training camp I was tiptoeing around because I didn't want to get him mad. Then I said 'Well, I can't not be myself anymore. So I started acting wild and young and crazy. And he enjoyed it. He needed it. At that time he didn't have the enthusiasm he had when he first came in. I think I helped him smile more."

The Magic Man has brought a lot of smiles to the faces of Laker fans. With him on the scene L.A. has won NBA titles in 1980, 1982, 1985, 1987, and 1988.

His great ball control and passing ability puts him in another dimension out there on the court. He led the league in assists in 1983, 1984, 1986, and 1987, and finally, late last year, he passed the all-time assists leader, Oscar Robertson. Magic had already passed Bob Cousy, Guy Rodgers, and Lenny Wilkens, the next three guys on the list. Quite an accomplishment, I'd say.

"It's hard to believe I'm in the company of guys like Bob Cousy and Guy Rodgers. I never saw them play, but I know about them. I know they were creative, throwing behind-the-back passes before they were common. I would have liked to have played with them." They would have liked to have played with Magic the way Byron Scott, Johnson's teammate, has liked it.

"Magic has the same enthusiasm now," says Scott, "that he always had. Playing with him? It's been an experience just knowing him. The enthusiasm for the game, the energy. It spreads through the court and off the court. He's a unique person. There isn't anybody in the league who has the enthusiasm and love for the game that Magic Johnson has."

What is special about Magic Johnson is his ability to motivate his teammates, to lead by example. The Lakers have been one of the most dominant teams of all time with him in the lineup—but without him there, what kind of team would they have been?

The Lakers win because of talent, but they win especially because of Magic Johnson. Whether it's passing, shooting, rebounding, stealing the ball, racking up assists, playing defense, or just inspiring his team-mates—he's always there.

"When I'm at work," Magic has said, "I'm going a hundred miles an hour . . . trying to win."

In basketball circles today there is a running debate as to who is the best player in the NBA: Michael Jordan, Magic Johnson, or Larry Bird. I'm not going to go out on that limb. I'll let Larry Bird have the last word. He calls Magic the best. "Magic makes his teammates better to a greater degree than I do," says Bird. "It's his character, not just his ability."

JORDAN

Michael Jordan is not like any player I've ever seen. Phil Jackson, one of my former players on the Knicks and now the head coach of the Chicago Bulls, says that "Jordan's a guy from another planet." I won't go that far, but Jordan is definitely the most entertaining player in the game today. Not only is he entertaining to the fans, but he also gets results for himself and his team. He's definitely a franchise player.

Michael's a combination of a lot of things, but his most important asset is his athletic ability. Jordan has amazing physical ability, total control of his body, and great jumping ability at different heights. They call him "Air Jordan" and "Rubber-Band Man" for good reason. It's like Wayne Embry said: "He plays higher than any-body's ever played."

Other players like Oscar Robertson, Elgin Baylor, Earl Monroe were great, but they were more methodical. Jordan has taken things to another level—constantly in-novating, making up shots and moves as he hangs in the air. And it happens on a nightly basis with him.

"I'm not sure myself what I'm going to be doing

once I'm up there," he says. "That's when instinct takes over, that's when the mind goes into its creativity." He's not just a jump shooter, so you can't get away with putting a big guy on him in hopes that he'll have difficulty in getting his shot off. Once those guys descend to the ground—and they always do—Jordan is still in the air. Michael can put the ball on the floor, and once he gets momentum going, no matter how great the defensive player is, it's pretty tough to stop Jordan from scoring. He has great desire, and supreme confidence in what he's doing.

Some people look at him as just an offensive player. Well, he certainly is that. For the last five seasons he's led the NBA in scoring, and I guess when you score the way he does—those back-to-back 50-point games in the playoffs in 1987–88, the first time *anyone* had ever done that—you get that kind of reputation.

Some say he forces things a lot of times. But I think with the teams he's been on, he's had to force things. But he can also make the pass, play defense, and rebound if he has to. People don't even notice that he's led the league in steals twice, that he's blocked over 100 shots twice, and that there were quite a few games where he made the game-winning defensive play. He's also very durable, and he plays hard all the time. In four of his first five seasons he averaged nearly 40 minutes a game. He's in the prime of his career—with seven seasons in the book—and there's no telling how great he can still become and how successful the Bulls become if they add the right people to help him out. Each year he's been with the Bulls they've gotten better. The scary thing for the rest of the NBA is that Michael Jordan has also gotten better. They finally won it all last year, and naturally he was the Finals MVP.

The Michael Jordan resume is a thing that a Hall of Famer is made of: NBA Most Valuable Player 1988 and 1991, Defensive Player of the Year 1988, led NBA in steals 1988 and 1990, NBA All Star Game Most Valuable Player 1988, NBA playoff-game record for most points (63) against Boston, April 20, 1986, etc., etc.

The man they call "Air Jordan" was born on February 17, 1963, in Brooklyn but moved down to play his high school ball at Laney in Wilmington, North Carolina. He led the University of North Carolina to the NCAA Division I championship in 1982, was a member of our gold-medal Olympic team in 1984, and was drafted that year by the Bulls as an undergraduate—the third pick in the NBA draft. For Michael it's been all excel and acceleration in the world of basketball. Every team he's played for has been made into a better team because of him.

In 1987–88, the Bulls put together a 50-32 record, their best in 14 years. It was a 10-game improvement in wins over their previous season and gave Chicago the third-best record in the Eastern Conference. Jordan lit their fire, scoring 2,868 points, recording a 35.0 average, playing 3,311 minutes, and stealing the ball 259 times—all league-leading stats. It was the finest year of his career.

"I want to win," Michael said. "I want to have fun and I want to entertain people." That he does. In 1987–88, for the second straight year, Jordan racked up more than 200 steals and 100 blocked shots—the only player in NBA history to ever accomplish that.

Not only is Michael Jordan a franchise player, he's an impact player, and a guy who's still improving. And there are many who think he may be the greatest ever to play the game. It was great to finally see him in the Finals last year, and he lived up to everyone's expectations. He did everything—score, pass, steal, defend, and most important, lead.

"Jordan is the ultimate go-to guy," says Detroit Pistons coach Chuck Daly. "He's superhuman. I don't know how he does it, where he gets that energy, his intelligence, his instinct for the game. It's like Philadelphia when Julius Erving was there. I'm telling the people of Chicago: You're seeing something that only comes around once in a lifetime. So enjoy it."

Larry Bird says, "I think he is God disguised as Michael Jordan. He is the most awesome player in the NBA." And Magic Johnson adds, "Michael's like a seven-footer because he can jump so high. Really, there is Michael Jordan and there's everybody else."

BAYLOR

The guy's stats are amazing:

Named to NBA 35th Anniversary All-Time Team; elected to the Basketball Hall of Fame; named to the NBA All Star First Team 1959, 1960, 1961, 1962, 1963, 1964, 1965, 1967, 1968, 1969; NBA Rookie of the Year 1959; led NCAA Division I in rebounding, 1957; NCAA University Division tournament MVP, 1958. And that's just part of the story.

Born on September 16, 1934, in Washington, D.C., Elgin Gay Baylor was selected out of Seattle University by the Minneapolis Lakers in 1958 in the first round of the NBA draft as a junior eligible. At Seattle he had averaged 32.5 points a game in his final year there.

Baylor was a shot in the arm to a franchise that needed help. Actually, then Laker president Bob Short had an even more dramatic version of the story. "If he had turned me down then," said Short, "I'd have gone out of business, the club would have gone bankrupt." So I guess Elgin was not only a franchise player but a franchise saver.

His importance to the Laker franchise was shown when John Kundla, who had all those great years as a coach for the franchise, was replaced by John Castellani, Baylor's college coach at Seattle.

Baylor finished fourth in the league in scoring as a rookie and started in the All Star Game. At 6'5" he amazed people by leaping up above the giants to snatch rebounds, but his forte was putting the ball into the hoop.

In a game against the Celtics in 1959, he scored 64 points on 25-for-36 shooting from the field and 14 free throws. Those 64 points broke the record of 63 points in a game set ten years before by Joe Fulks. The Celtics started to stall late in the game to keep Baylor's scoring down. They even put three guys on him. That didn't do too much good. Leading his Lakers to victory over Boston was a double treat for the small Minneapolis crowd. There were only 2,001 fans in the Minneapolis Auditorium. But all of them took satisfaction in the fact that the Lakers' 136-113 win over Boston broke a 22-game losing streak that went back all the way to March 1957.

His ability to hang in the air, his great body control, the tremendous strength and spring in his legs, that incredible creativity in improvising shots—those things made Baylor almost impossible to stop. Today there is Michael Jordan, Dominque Wilkins, Clyde Drexler—players with all the moves. But when Baylor came along he was one of the first of that type, which led to much of the concept of team defense and double teaming that we see today.

I can still remember him taking the ball off the defensive backboard and streaking upcourt on a one-man fast break, making those change-of-pace dribbles, accelerating quickly and going to the basket. Elgin was so big and strong at 6'5" and 225 pounds that he would hang in the air and wait to get fouled. He wanted to get whacked and usually wouldn't shoot the ball until he felt that he was getting hit. When he shot, he usually made the basket and the free throw and wound up with a three-point play.

The Lakers of Minneapolis became the Lakers of Los Angeles in the 1960–61 season. There were only 3,000 fans at that first Laker game. But there would be more, many more, later on. The great draw was Elgin Baylor—not only for his scoring and rebounding but because of his razzle-dazzle style of play. He was a great gate attraction.

There were also so many nights that he led the Lakers in what he called his "hat trick." That was leading the team in points, rebounds, and assists.

The team he seemed to really get up for was the Boston Celtics. On April 14, 1962, Baylor scored 61 points in the fifth game of the title series against the Celtics—the most points to that time by a player in an NBA Finals game. He also scored 71 points in a regular-season game against the New York Knickerbockers in 1960, but I'm not going to dwell on that . . .

One of the great compliments a player could receive in Baylor's time was to be compared to him. Scouts and coaches would say, "Plays like Baylor, shoots like Baylor, rebounds like Baylor, has the heart of Baylor." Those were all comparisons. The original model was in a class by itself—all heart, all talent, all drive. Elgin Baylor was an impact player, one of the greatest forwards of all time, a true franchise player.

ABDUL-JABBAR

The way time passes and the way all of life is kind of a continuum was made really clear to me in November of 1988. I was at Madison Square Garden watching Kareem Abdul-Jabbar making the first of his appearances in his final NBA tour.

I wondered about the times I used to play handball against Kareem's father at Franklin K. Lane High School. I thought about the times when Kareem was a player and he used to kid me when I was a coach that his father was a better handball player than me. I thought of the hours and hours I spent reviewing films of Kareem in action and how I planned ways to keep him under control when he was a player on the Milwaukee Bucks and then the Los Angeles Lakers and my teams had to go up against him.

In his farewell appearance at Madison Square Garden Kareem said, "I hope people appreciate what I was able to do, and the fact that I was able to do it consistently. You know, I think there was a conscious effort to minimize what I did, and because of that, my appreciation by the public suffered. But there's nothing that can be done about that, and I'm not concerned about it . . . I'm not concerned."

Kareem shouldn't be concerned. In my book he's one of the great franchise players of all time. And like Old Man River, he just kept rolling along through 20 grueling NBA seasons, outlasting everyone to become at age forty-two the oldest guy ever to play in the league.

His stats are staggering: leading all-time scorer, most games played, most minutes played, most field goals made, most field goals attempted, most blocked shots, etc.—the list goes on and on.

During his prime, Kareem was probably the best all-around center the game has ever seen. He was a combination of some of the best qualities of Bill Russell and Wilt Chamberlain. He had the height, the reach, and at times the scoring ability of Wilt, and he had the speed and the defense of Russell. Like Bill, Kareem also had the ability to run the court and make the pass.

A dream player for a coach to have, Kareem always gave an honest day's work and never stopped trying to improve his game. And he just kept getting better and better as a basketball player as his career went on. Highly intelligent, a true team player, an unselfish guy, he always made those around him play better. Magic Johnson, great as he is, credits Kareem with making him play at a higher level.

Out of Power Memorial in New York City and then after a great career at UCLA—he led John Wooden's Bruins to three NCAA championships—Kareem was the first pick in the 1969 NBA draft. They called him the "Million Dollar Buck" when he joined Milwaukee because of the salary he received.

All he did for his money was average 28.8 points a game in his rookie season and win the Rookie of the Year award. And all he did for the Bucks was to make a mediocre team into a good team and then a great team, leading them to the NBA championship in 1971.

Then after six years in Milwaukee, Kareem wanted to move on. The cold winters, the snow, a feeling of marking time, these were the reasons he gave for wanting out. On June 16, 1975, the Lakers and Bucks concluded a blockbuster trade. Kareem went to L.A. and Milwaukee acquired Elmore Smith, Brian Winters, Dave Meyers, and Junior Bridgeman, and a million dollars. Looking back on that deal it was one of the biggest steals in NBA trading history.

The Knicks could have topped that package, and Kareem could have played for me and owned New York City. But it never was able to happen. Although Kareem's been quoted as saying that he wanted to play in New York "but unfortunately the Knicks did not have the determination to make the deal," that wasn't true. We wanted Kareem, wanted him badly, and we tried to get him. Someone sold him a bill of goods that we weren't interested, but we were, very, very interested. Imagine what the course of basketball history might have been if he had wound up playing for me and the Knicks?"

But I didn't have Kareem—I only had my own problems thinking of ways for my guys to handle him. In his early years in the league one of the tactics that worked with some success was having a player like Willis Reed use his superior strength to push on Kareem so that he'd be out of position for a shot. That physical routine worked for us during Kareem's early years, but as he got older, stronger, and smarter, the approach didn't work as well.

It was always really very difficult to defend against him. His feel for the game, his curiosity about the game, his instinct for the game, in addition to all the other things he had going for him, made him a great player.

And Kareem also had the sky hook—the shot that Magic Johnson said "is what's a lay-in to anybody else. It's money." The sky hook, the specialty of Kareem Abdul-Jabbar, made its debut when he was nine years old.

"With a guy from the other team at my back," he explained about the shot's origin, "I looked over my shoulder, saw the basket, turned in the lane and with one hand put up my first hook shot. It missed, hit the back rim and bounced out. But it felt right, and the next time I got the ball I tried it again. Neither of them went in, but I had found my shot."

His discovery of that shot proved to be bad news for the hundreds of guys that came up against Kareem. That shot has been one of the most amazing offensive weapons in basketball history. Right-handed or left-handed, a knee going up, the ball held so high in the hand that it seemed he was shooting down at the basket in an arc high above all the other arms out there on the court, then that *plunk* as the ball dropped into the basket—that was his ritual through thousands of games.

What made the shot so tough to defend against was the way Kareem used his agility to move away from the basket and out of the reach of the guy guarding him. Even players his size couldn't stop the shot. And he was always so intelligent out there that when he was caught out of position for the shot, he rarely ever forced it up there. At 7'2", head up, Kareem was always looking over players to spot the open man and hit him with a pass.

Named the NBA's Most Valuable Player five times in his first seven years in the league, a member of five Los Angeles Laker championship teams, a ten-time first-team NBA All Star, Kareem Abdul-Jabbar was the franchise for the Lakers.

As his last coach, Pat Riley, said, "In his prime he was the most dominating player in the game. And he had a tremendous burden because he was expected to do more than anybody in the league—score, rebound, block shots, lead the team."

The kid born as Lew Alcindor on April 16, 1947, in New York City, who used to swim in Far Rockaway where his father was a lifeguard, who was a youthful fan of the New York Knicks and the Brooklyn Dodgers, now belongs to the record books and to the memories of all of us who saw him play.

As Kareem has said, "The sport definitely goes on. People find new heroes, new people to admire. I'm flattered that they'll have to compare them with me."

REED

The date was May 8, 1970. The place was Madison Square Garden. The event was my New York Knicks against the Los Angeles Lakers in the seventh and final game of the NBA championship series. It was our 38th sellout of the season. I was ready. The crowd was ready. The Lakers were ready. The Knicks were ready. But no one knew if Willis Reed was ready.

A banged-up knee had made him miss part of Game Five and kept him out of Game Six. The doctors said it was up to Willis to decide if he could give it a go in Game Seven. I asked him if he could play.

"There's still some soreness," Willis told me, "but I can do it."

"Swell, I'll start you."

"Get some more heat for that leg," Dr. Parkes, our team doctor, advised Willis, "and get some rest."

No one in the crowd knew what had been decided. No one knew that Willis was going to try to play. John Condon, the public-address announcer, gave the crowd our starting lineup. Dave DeBusschere and Bill Bradley got big ovations. But when Condon made the announcement: "At center, Captain Willis Reed," the crowd stood

and roared, and the roof in the Garden seemed to trem-
ble. The noise went on for almost a minute. It was a good
thing Condon still had to introduce Walt Frazier and
Dick Barnett. That got the crowd to sit down. But they
were up all the way.

Willis Reed and Wilt Chamberlain lined up for the
tip-off. Wilt went high, and Willis barely left his feet. It
was painful for him just to move about. L.A. got the tap.
Baylor missed a jump shot from the side. DeBusschere
rebounded, and we went on the offense.

Willis, moving with the skip of a peg-legged guy, was
the last man downcourt. He set up behind the foul line.
Chamberlain dropped away from him. A flat-footed
Reed hit a 15-footer, and we drew first blood. And the
crowd, roaring, was into it.

Ninety seconds later we had a 4-2 lead. Willis set up
in the right corner about twenty feet from the basket.
Again Chamberlain dropped off him. Frazier got the ball
to Willis, who shot and hit. The crowd was in a frenzy,
and so were the guys on our bench.

Although Willis was banged up and could have and
maybe should have watched the game from a bed in
his hotel room, he wanted to play. His presence and his
couple of baskets right at the start were the things that
brought the crowd into the game early. The Garden
rocked and rolled with emotion as our fans took their
lead from Willis. They were willing us to win just as he
was willing himself to play. Although he played only 27
minutes and scored just those four points, his presence
was the big story.

Going into the last six minutes, we led 106-81. Bed-
lam was on parade in the Garden. People were standing
up and shouting, "We're Number One!"

We were number one. At the end, we beat the Lakers 113-99 to bring the first NBA championship in history to New York City.

Afterwards Walt Frazier told a reporter, "Just the presence of Willis was the turning point in the game. To see him come out, to see him with his two baskets . . . We were worried, man. A couple of guys tried to tell jokes before we came out but nothing was funny."

The Knicks had been in business since 1946, and this first championship had been a long time coming. It was touching for me to be the coach of that team. And it was something to have all those great and intelligent players doing their thing. But Willis Reed, the captain, was the impact player, the franchise. What he did, offensively, defensively, was a given. How he was able to be the soul of that team was made clear in the seventh game of that battle against the L.A. Lakers for the 1969–70 NBA Championship.

Not too many people remember that Willis Reed was a second-round draft pick in 1964. The more I read over that sentence, the more amazing it seems that Willis lasted till the second round. I first came into contact with Willis when he played for Grambling College. That wasn't too far from his hometown in Bernice, Louisiana. I was a scout for the Knicks back in the early sixties and spent a good deal of my time at Grambling, then the top black college for athletics in the United States.

Sitting in the Grambling gym and watching Willis in action, I realized he was an unfinished product. Out there on the court, he was kind of raw. But he was an exceptional shooter. One of the things that I especially liked about Willis was his ability to get and hold position under the basket and block other guys out. That weight and strength was amazing. And I knew they would be assets for Willis as a great pro center.

When the draft finally took place, those of us who had to make the big decisions on the Knicks went back and forth trying to figure out who to choose. Willis, Jim "Bad News" Barnes of Texas Western, and Lucious Jackson of Pan American were the guys we projected as number-one draft choices. The Knicks picked Barnes in the first round. Jackson was taken by Philadelphia. And when the first round ended, incredibly, Willis Reed was still available. The Boston Celtics had the final pick in the first round. And they passed Willis by. When our turn came up again in the second round, we grabbed Willis.

Life is like that. Somebody once wrote a poem about the road not taken. They could also write one about the player not picked. Had the Celtics gotten Willis Reed, there's no telling how many basketball championships they might have won, and they won plenty. Had the Knicks not wound up with Willis Reed, I don't know if I would have won those two championships with the Knicks, and you probably wouldn't be reading this book.

Willis Reed was one of the most coachable players I ever knew. When he first joined the Knicks, he asked me for an NBA rulebook. He was the only one I can recall who ever asked for one. Willis was a student of the game right from the start. Toughness and an incredible tolerance for pain were parts of his makeup. There were a few times when Willis had his nose broken in games. If that's ever happened to you, you know how painful that is. Each time Willis's nose was broken, he went back to the bench and told our trainer, Danny Whelan, "Pop it back in, Danny." Danny obliged, and Willis played on.

The guy was a leader. We'd room him with rookies, and he would take them under his wing, show them the ropes, get them plugged into the whys and wherefores of being a professional basketball player. In practice, Willis set a very good example. He would work his butt off. Whether the stuff he had to do was boring or interesting, he put the same great effort forward.

Not too many people know that although Willis Reed was listed at 6'10", he was only 6'8". That meant he gave away several inches to other centers like Wilt Chamberlain. But Willis played big. And he made up for the inches because his heart was inches bigger than most of the guys he came up against.

I had so many great players on my championship Knicks: Earl Monroe, Bill Bradley, Walt Frazier, Dick Barnett, Dave DeBusschere, Jerry Lucas . . . but Willis, who is in the Hall of Fame along with most of the others, was much more than a great player. He was the only true franchise player among them.

I left a few guys out of my in-depth list of franchise players because their careers have not yet gotten them to the stage where they've been able to have the full impact that I expect them to have.

But Hakeem Olajuwon, David Robinson, and Charles Barkley look to me like they'll also wind up as true franchise players. They dominate. It's tough to dominate them. And they make their teammates better, too.

A sure bet for the next franchise player is Patrick Ewing—and he just might be there already. When the Knicks selected him as the number-one pick in the lottery, everybody predicted that Patrick would be the franchise. It's taken him a couple of years to really show his stuff. But now Patrick's really coming on. He's worked hard at learning the transition from the college game to the pro game. The extra weight, strength, and endurance he's developed has helped his overall game. When Pat first came into the league, he would pick up a lot of silly fouls and would also try to do everything by himself out on the court—play defense, rebound, take charge.

Now he plays much more under control. With his height, strength, agility, intelligence, and desire, there's no telling how great Pat Ewing will become. He's already made the players around him better players. And he's the guy all the other teams try to control. In the way Pat impacts on a game he reminds of Willis Reed. And he may become to today's Knicks what Willis was to my teams—the franchise.

10
Red's Quizzes

You've got to be a real diehard basketball fan to be plowing through all this stuff. So, for a change of pace, I thought you'd enjoy giving your "Hoop I.Q." a workout. Here are a few quizzes that should give you a run for the money.

QUIZ #1:
THE NBA

1. This guy was a star third baseman during the thirties with the New York Yankees. But he was also one of four head coaches of the Toronto Huskies during the '46–47 season. (By the way, he was a far better baseball player than he ever was a basketball coach.) Who was he?

2. Everybody knows that Red Auerbach has won the most games as a coach in NBA history. Most of those wins came with the Boston Celtics. But he coached two other teams before he came to Boston. Names those teams.

3. Still on Auerbach, Red joined the Celtics in their fifth season. Name the two coaches who were with Boston before him.

4. This is a two-part question. This team had the worst record in NBA history: 9 and 73, appropriately during the '72–73 season (for those of you who are into numbers). Name the team, and name the two different coaches it had that year.

5. Now, another two-part question: Speaking of two coaches, only two coaches ever won championships in both the NBA and the ABA. You know your basketball if you can name them and the teams they coached.

6. Who was the original coach of the San Antonio Spurs? Big hint: I coached the guy once. Bigger hint: His initials are C.H. That's all you're getting on this question.

7. A question for old-timers: A regular catcher for the St. Louis Cardinals played with the Rochester Royals during their National Basketball League years. Hint: His initials were D.R.

8. Here's an easy one: Who has the longest consecutive game-playing streak in NBA history? Hint: I coached him and helped him get the record by playing him. Bonus question: How many games were in the streak?

9. Only two guys were ever picked as co-winners of the NBA Rookie-of-the-Year Award. Name the players and their teams.

10. Back in 1962, Wilt Chamberlain was unbelievable. The big guy averaged an incredible 48.5 minutes per game. He was a horse. His backup hardly got any playing time at center, but got some minutes at forward. Name Mr. Anonymous.

11. Kareem Abdul-Jabbar now holds the record as the oldest player in NBA history. Who held it before? (This is a trick question, but the guy who held it was tricky with the basketball.)

12. This one is for those of you who were American Basketball Association fans. Name the eleven original teams in the ABA in the '67–68 season. (If you get half of these, you know your basketball.)

13. Speaking of names, what cities had NBA franchises with the following nicknames: Stags, Rebels, Falcons, Bombers, and Redskins?

14. Here's a father-and-son team that you should know. The father played on the first NBA championship team, the '46–47 Philadelphia Warriors. The son coached in the NBA. Name them. Well, I'll make it easy on you. Just give me their last name. (Actually, I'm not making it that easy because they both had the same first name.)

15. Here's another question on old-time basketball. (If you've been reading this book carefully, you'll realize I gave this answer earlier.) An early professional team was named for a dance hall in which it played. Name the team.

Answers at end of chapter

QUIZ #2:
THE ABA

This quiz is especially for you people who were American Basketball Association fans.

1. I'll start you off with an easy one. What team won the most ABA championships and how many did this team win?

2. This is a toughie, and only real basketball junkies will probably get it right. It's a two-part question. If you get either part right, you're a winner. When and where was the first ABA game ever played?

3. Maybe this is the toughest question in the book. Who scored the first basket in ABA history? Hint: It had to be a guy who played in that game.

4. The red, white, and blue basketball is famous; some would say infamous. One guy generally gets the credit for introducing it into the ABA. Who is the guy? Hint: His initials are G.M.

5. Easy question: Name the first ABA scoring champion.

6. Follow-up question: What team did Connie play for when he led the league in scoring that first ABA season?

7. The New York Nets, during their first eight years in the ABA, played in six arenas in the New York

metropolitan area during regular- and post-season play. Now, I don't expect you to name all six. If you can name three, you make the All-Holzman team. If you can name at least one, you make my co-author's team.

8. This question comes under the "unbelievable but true" category. I'll make it multiple choice to give you a fighting chance. What is the ABA record for the least number of points scored by a team in a single quarter of a game? Choices: a) 2; b) 6; c) 8; d) 9; e) 13.

9. The Memphis franchise was nicknamed the "Tams." I know you knew that. But how did they get that nickname?

10. That Memphis franchise had two other nicknames in addition to "Tams." If you get both other names, you're on the All-Holzman team. If you get just one of the names, you've got to settle for being on my co-author's club.

11. This should be an easy one for you. Two guys led the ABA in scoring and also were the scoring leaders of other professional leagues. Name the guys and the leagues.

12. This question is not as tough as it seems. The ABA, in its history, had six commissioners and one interim commissioner. If you name three or less, you know whose team you go on, and if you name four or more, you're on my team.

13. Name the guy who holds the ABA record for most rebounds in a season. Hint: His initials are S.H. Double hint: I once coached the guy.

14. Everybody knows the ABA had a tough time. But three charter members of the league finished their existence in the same cities that they began when the ABA first came into existence. Name those three charter members who survived nine ABA seasons.

15. If this ABA quiz wore you out, we'll end it with an easy question. Name the guy who owned an ABA team, a major league baseball team, and a national hockey league at the same time.

The American Basketball Association is a footnote to sports history. Coaching in the NBA, I used to look over my shoulder at the Nets and the other teams that played in that league. So here's a tip of the hat to the players, who had something to prove, the owners, some of whom lost their shirts, and the fans, who were treated to wide-open and sometimes adventurous basketball in arenas all over the United States.

Answers at end of chapter

QUIZ #3:
THE NBL

This quiz is for guys who have been following basketball for a long time, like my agent, Artie Pine. If you get more than half the answers right, you qualify as a hoop genius.

1. I figured some variety in the quizzes would make things interesting. This question will require you to match the nicknames of the teams to the cities they played in in the NBA.

   a) Youngstown, Ohio   1) Duffey Packers

   b) Oshkosh, Wisconsin   2) American Gears

   c) Anderson, Indiana   3) Nationals

   d) Chicago, Illinois   4) Jeeps

   e) Waterloo, Iowa   5) Bears

   f) Syracuse, New York   6) Hawks

   g) Toledo, Ohio   7) All-Stars

   h) Sheboygan, Wisconsin   8) Redskins

2. Now we'll try your hand at fill-ins. _____ was the last year of the NBL, and the _____ were the last NBL champion. Bonus: _____ was the last NBL Rookie of the Year.

3. Here's an easy one. Name the team that played in the Edgerton Park Sports Arena.

The next three questions are identifications.

4. This guy made his name in pro football, but he also played on a championship NBL team.

5. This guy owned a supermarket and also owned and coached an NBL team that was named for him.

6. This guy was a Seton Hall all-American who played with me on the Rochester Royals.

7. Here's a tough one. This guy played for Cleveland and was the first to average over 20 points a game in the NBL in a season. Hint: His initials are M.R., and he turned the trick in 1944–45.

8. What team won three straight NBL titles?

9. The Atlanta Hawks of the NBA traces their roots back to the NBL. What NBL team was the great-grandaddy of the Hawks? If you've been reading this book carefully, you'll remember I gave you this answer in my section on team nicknames.

Answers at end of chapter

QUIZ ANSWERS

QUIZ #1:
THE NBA

1. Robert "Red" Rolfe.

2. the Washington Capitols and the Tri-Cities Hawks.

3. John "Honey" Russell and Alvin "Dogie" Julian.

4. Philadelphia '76ers, Roy Rubin and Kevin Loughery.

5. Alex Hannum with the '69 Oakland Oaks, the '58 St. Louis Hawks, and the '67 Philadelphia 76ers; Bill Sharman with the '71 Utah Stars and the '72 L.A. Lakers.

6. Cliff Hagan.

7. Del Rice.

8. Randy Smith, 906.

9. Dave Cowens of Boston and Geoff Petrie of Portland.

10. Joe Ruklick

11. Bob Cousy. Seven years after his 1963 retirement, he played in seven games for the Cincinnati Royals. He was forty-one at the time, and the Royals' coach.

12. Anaheim Amigos, Dallas Chaparrals, Denver Rockets, Houston Mavericks, Indiana Pacers, Kentucky

Colonels, Minnesota Muskies, New Jersey Americans, New Orleans Buccaneers, Oakland Oaks, Pittsburgh Pipers.

13. Chicago, Cleveland, Detroit, St. Louis, Sheboygan.

14. Guokas (first name: Matt).

15. the New York Rens, originally known as the Harlem Renaissance Five, named for the Renaissance Casino Ballroom in Harlem.

QUIZ #2:
THE ABA

1. Indiana Pacers, 3.

2. October 13, 1967, was the date. It was a game played at the Oakland Coliseum. The Oaks beat the Anaheim Amigos.

3. Willie Porter of Oakland.

4. George Mikan, the league's first commissioner.

5. Connie Hawkins.

6. Pittsburgh Pipers.

7. Teaneck Armory in Teaneck, New Jersey; the Long Island Arena in Commack, Long Island; the Island Garden in West Hempstead, Long Island; the Nassau Coliseum in Uniondale, Long Island; Madison Square Garden—you know where that is; and the

Felt Forum. No, I didn't trick you, the Felt Forum is a 5,000-seat arena that's part of the Madison Square Garden complex.

8. c) 8—It happened four times to four different teams.

9. Memphis got the name "Tams" because of its geographical position on the Mississippi River at the conjunction of Tennessee, Arkansas, and Missouri.

10. Memphis "Pros" and Memphis "Sounds."

11. Rick Barry and Connie Hawkins. Barry led both the NBA and ABA, while Hawkins led the ABA and the American Basketball League (ABL).

12. George Mikan, Jack Dolph, Robert Carlson, Mike Storen, Tedd Munchak, Dave DeBusschere. The interim commissioner was Jim Garden.

13. Spencer Haywood.

14. Denver, Indiana, and Kentucky.

15. Charles O. Finley.

QUIZ #3:
THE NBL

1. a–5; b–7; c–1; d–2; e–6; f–3; g–4; h–8.

2. 1948–49; Anderson Packers; Dolph Schayes.

3.   My old team, the Rochester Royals.

4.   Otto Graham.

5.   Frank Kautsky. The Indianapolis Kautskys were his team.

6.   Bob Davies.

7.   Mel Riebe.

8.   the Fort Wayne Pistons, 1942–45.

9.   Buffalo in 1946 became the Tri-Cities Blackhawks, then the Milwaukee Hawks, then the St. Louis Hawks, then the Atlanta Hawks.

11

Red's Lists

For trivia buffs, stat guys, and all of you concerned with hoop oddities, this part of the book, courtesy of the NBA, is for you.

FIRST SEASONS OF EXPANSION TEAMS

NBA expansion teams never have had an easy time of it in their inaugural seasons. Not counting the four clubs which were taken in from the ABA in 1976, the NBA's 15 expansion teams since 1961 have averaged 20.7 wins in their first year. The 1967 Chicago Bulls, coached by Johnny Kerr, posted a high of 33 wins while the low of 15 was notched by four clubs—the 1968 San Diego Rockets under Jack McMahon, the 1971 Cleveland Cavaliers under Bill Fitch, the 1981 Dallas Mavericks under Dick Motta, and the 1989 Miami Heat under Ron Rothstein. Here's a look at the first seasons of past expansion teams:

Season	Team	Won	Lost	Pct.
1990	Orlando Magic	18	64	.220
1990	Minnesota Timberwolves	22	60	.268
1989	Miami Heat	15	67	.183
1989	Charlotte Hornets	20	62	.244

Season	Team	Won	Lost	Pct.
1981	Dallas Mavericks	15	67	.183
1975	New Orleans Jazz	23	59	.280
1971	Portland Trail Blazers	29	53	.354
1971	Buffalo Braves	22	60	.268
1971	Cleveland Cavaliers	15	67	.183
1969	Milwaukee Bucks	27	55	.329
1969	Phoenix Suns	16	66	.195
1968	Seattle SuperSonics	23	59	.280
1968	San Diego Rockets	15	67	.183
1967	Chicago Bulls	33	48	.407
1962	Chicago Packers	18	62	.225

U.S. OLYMPIANS WHO HAVE PLAYED IN THE NBA

1948
Cliff Barker
Don Barksdale
Ralph Beard
Vince Boryla
Alex Groza
Wallace Jones
Ray Lumpp
Ken Rollins

1952
Clyde Lovellette

1956
K. C. Jones
Bill Russell
Jim Walsh

1960
Jay Arnette
Walt Bellamy
Bob Boozer
Terry Dischinger
Darrall Imhoff
Jerry Lucas
Oscar Robertson
Adrian Smith
Jerry West

1964
Jim Barnes
Bill Bradley
Joe Caldwell
Mel Counts
Walt Hazard
Lucious Jackson
Jeff Mullins
George Wilson

1968
Spencer Haywood
Bill Hosket
Charlie Scott
Mike Silliman
Jo Jo White

1972
Mike Bantom
Jim Brewer
Tom Burleson
Doug Collins
Tom Henderson
Bobby Jones
Dwight Jones
Tom McMillen
Ed Ratleff

1976

Tate Armstrong
Quinn Buckner
Kenny Carr
Adrian Dantley
Walter Davis
Phil Ford
Ernie Grunfeld
Phil Hubbard
Mitch Kupchak
Tom LaGarde
Scott May
Steve Sheppard

1980

Mark Aguirre
Rolando Blackman
Sam Bowie
Michael Brooks
Bill Hanzlik
Alton Lister
Rodney McCray
Isiah Thomas
Darnell Valentine
Danny Vranes

Buck Williams
Al Wood

1984

Steve Alford
Patrick Ewing
Vern Fleming
Michael Jordan
Joe Kleine
Jon Koncak
Chris Mullin
Sam Perkins
Alvin Robertson
Wayman Tisdale
Jeff Turner
Leon Wood

1988

Willie Anderson
Jeff Grayer
Hersey Hawkins
Dan Majerle
Danny Manning
Mitch Richmond
Charles Smith

THE 2,000-500-500 CLUB

Only four players in NBA history have had at least 2,000 points, 500 rebounds, and 500 assists in the same season —Oscar Robertson, John Havlicek, Larry Bird, and Michael Jordan. Robertson has done it six times, Bird three, and Havlicek and Jordan two.

Player	Season	Points	Rebounds	Assists
Michael Jordan	1990	2,753	565	519
Michael Jordan	1989	2,633	652	650
Larry Bird	1987	2076	682	566
Larry Bird	1986	2,115	805	557
Larry Bird	1985	2,295	842	531
John Havlicek	1972	2,252	672	614
John Havlicek	1971	2,338	730	607

Player	Season	Points	Rebounds	Assists
Oscar Robertson	1966	2,378	586	847
Oscar Robertson	1965	2,279	674	861
Oscar Robertson	1964	2,480	783	868
Oscar Robertson	1963	2,264	835	758
Oscar Robertson	1962	2,432	985	899
Oscar Robertson	1961	2,165	716	690

GREAT ROOKIE SEASONS

Since the NBA began in 1946, only 49 players have averaged as many as 20 points in their first season. (Eighteen of those rookie seasons were in the American Basketball Association.) Here are the eleven greatest first seasons ever:

Player	Team	Year	FG%	Rebound Avg.	Scoring Avg.
Wilt Chamberlain	Philadelphia	1959–60	.461	26.9	37.6
Walt Bellamy	Chicago	1961–62	.519	19.0	31.6
Oscar Robertson	Cincinnati	1960–61	.473	10.1	30.5
Dan Issel	Kentucky (ABA)	1970–71	.470	13.2	29.9
Kareem Abdul-Jabbar	Milwaukee	1969–70	.518	14.5	28.8
Elvin Hayes	San Diego	1968–69	.447	17.1	28.4
Michael Jordan	Chicago	1984–85	.515	6.5	28.2
Julius Erving	Virginia (ABA)	1971–72	.498	15.7	27.3
David Thompson	Denver (ABA)	1975–76	.515	6.3	26.0
David Robinson	San Antonio	1989–90	.531	12.0	24.3
Larry Bird	Boston	1979–80	.474	10.4	21.3

THE 30-10 CLUB

In 1989–90, Karl Malone became the first player since Moses Malone in 1982 to average 30 points and 10 rebounds in the same season. Remember, since shooting averages have risen over the past thirty years, rebounds have gotten increasingly scarce, so it's quite a feat. Here are the 23 times it's been done:

Year	Player	Points	Rebounds
1990	Karl Malone	31.0	11.1
1982	Moses Malone	31.1	14.7
1976	Bob McAdoo	31.1	12.4
1975	Kareem Abdul-Jabbar	30.0	14.0
	Bob McAdoo	35.4	14.1
1974	Bob McAdoo	30.6	15.1
1973	Kareem Abdul-Jabbar	30.2	16.1
1972	Kareem Abdul-Jabbar	34.8	16.6
1971	Kareem Abdul-Jabbar	31.7	16.0
1966	Wilt Chamberlain	33.5	24.6
1965	Wilt Chamberlain	34.7	22.9
1964	Wilt Chamberlain	36.9	22.3
1963	Elgin Baylor	34.0	14.3
	Wilt Chamberlain	44.8	24.3
1962	Walt Bellamy	31.6	19.0
	Wilt Chamberlain	50.4	25.7
	Bob Pettit	31.1	18.7
	Oscar Robertson	30.8	12.5
1961	Elgin Baylor	34.8	19.8
	Wilt Chamberlain	38.4	27.2
	Oscar Robertson	30.5	10.1
1960	Wilt Chamberlain	37.6	27.0

PROGRESS! PROGRESS!

Ten teams in NBA history have improved by 20 games or more in one season. Leading the way are the San Antonio Spurs of 1990, who improved by 35 games after adding a rookie by the name of David Robinson. Here are the clubs that made the most progress in one season:

Team	Seasons	First Year	Second Year	Improvement
San Antonio Spurs	1989–90	21-61	56-26	+35
Boston Celtics	1979–80	29-53	61-21	+32
Milwaukee Bucks	1969–70	27-55	56-26	+29
Phoenix Suns	1969–70	16-66	39-43	+23
San Diego Rockets	1968–69	15-67	37-45	+22
Baltimore Bullets	1968–69	36-46	57-25	+21

Team	Seasons	First Year	Second Year	Improvement
Buffalo Braves	1973–74	21-61	42-40	+21
LA Lakers	1971–72	48-34	69-13	+21
Chicago Bulls	1976–77	24-58	44-38	+20
New Jersey Nets	1981–82	24-58	44-38	+20

THREE! THREE! THREE!

The highest 3-point field-goal percentages in an NBA season:

FG%	Team	Year	Made-Attempted
.407	Cleveland	1989–90	346-851
.3844	Boston	1987–88	271-705
.384	Boston	1979–80	162–422

And the lowest 3-point field-goal percentages in an NBA season:

FG%	Team	Year	Made-Attempted
.104	L.A. Lakers	1982–83	10-96
.122	Atlanta	1980–81	10-82
.138	L.A. Lakers	1981–82	13-94

BEST STARTS

I take satisfaction in the fact that my 1970–71 Knicks still have the record for the best start in NBA history. Here are the best starts with one loss and the teams' final records:

Team	Season	Start	Final Record
New York Knicks	1969–70	23-1	60-22
Portland Trail Blazers	1990–91	18-1	63-19
Milwaukee Bucks	1970–71	17-1	66-16
Milwaukee Bucks	1971–72	17-1	63-19

Team	Season	Start	Final Record
Washington Capitols	1948–49	16-1	38-22
Syracuse Nationals	1949–50	16-1	51-13
St. Louis Hawks	1967–68	16-1	56-26
Boston Celtics	1957–58	15-1	49-23
Boston Celtics	1963–64	15-1	59-21
Philadelphia 76ers	1966–67	15-1	68-13
Milwaukee Bucks	1973–74	15-1	59-23

A THOUSAND VICTORIES

When the Chicago Bulls beat visiting Utah 99-89 on March 8 for their 1,000th victory, they became the tenth-fastest team in NBA history to reach that milestone. The Bulls reached 1,000 wins in 2,025 games, while Boston was the fastest in 1,593 games. Here's a list of NBA teams with 1,000 victories and the number of games it took them to reach the milestone:

Rank	Team	Games
1.	Boston	1,593
2.	Milwaukee	1,654
3.	Philadelphia	1,711
4.	L.A. Lakers	1,757
5.	Atlanta	1,855
6.	New York	1,976
7.	Washington	1,993
8.	Sacramento	2,009
9.	Golden State	2,017
10.	Chicago	2,025
11.	Detroit	2,216

IT RUNS IN THE FAMILY

Last year, there were 14 NBA players who had a brother playing at the NCAA Division I level:

NBA Player	College Player
*Larry Bird, Boston Celtics	Eddie Bird, Indiana State
Ledell Eackles, Washington Bullets	Marvin Eackles, South Alabama
Byron Irvin, Washington Bullets	Lance Irvin, Idaho
*Dave Jamerson, Houston Rockets	Tom Jamerson, Ohio
Stacey King, Chicago Bulls	Darryl King, Kansas State
*Dan Majerle, Phoenix Suns	Jeff Majerle, Central Michigan
*Chris Mullin, Golden State Warriors	Terence Mullin, St. John's
Larry Nance, Cleveland Cavaliers	Mike Nance, Charleston Southern
Akeem Olajuwon, Houston Rockets	Taju Olajuwon, Tex.-San Antonio
Walter Palmer, Utah Jazz	Crawford Palmer, Duke
*Chuck Person, Indiana Pacers	Wesley Person, Auburn
Mark Price, Cleveland Cavaliers	Brent Price, Oklahoma
*Fred Roberts, Milwaukee Bucks	Kenneth Roberts, Brigham Young
*David Robinson, San Antonio Spurs	Chuck Robinson, Navy

*Attended the same college as his younger brother.

COACHING IN COLLEGE

Last year, 15 of the 27 NBA head coaches previously had a similar job at a four-year college:

Coach, Team	College(s)	Record
Richie Adubalo, Mavericks	Upsala (N.Y.)	100- 62
Larry Brown, Spurs	UCLA, Kansas	171- 61
Chuck Daly, Pistons	Boston College, Penn	151- 62
Bill Fitch, Nets	Coe, N.D., BGSU, Minnesota	181-115
Cotton Fitzsimmons, Suns	Kansas State	34- 20
Del Harris, Bucks	Earlham (Ind.)	175- 70
K.C. Jones, SuperSonics	Brandeis (Mass.)	35- 32
Gene Littles, Hornets	North Carolina A&T	36- 15
Jim Lynam, 76ers	Fairfield, American, St. Joseph's	158-118
John MacLeod, Knicks	Oklahoma	80- 79
Dick Motta, Kings	Weber State	120- 33
Bill Musselman, Timberwolves	Ashland (O.), Minnesota	198- 62
Mike Schuler, Clippers	Virginia Military, Rice	43-139
Dick Versace, Pacers	Bradley	156- 88
Paul Westhead, Nuggets	La Salle, Loyola Marymount	247-153

BIGGER, OLDER, BETTER

In comparison to previous statistics, last year's NBA players were taller, heavier, older, and more experienced as a group. The average player was 6'7.16", weighed 216 pounds, was 27.01 years old, and had 4.08 seasons of prior NBA experience.

Here are the breakdowns by team:

			HEIGHT			
Rank	Team	Players	Total Inches	Average Height	Seven Footers	Rank 1989
1	San Antonio	12	966	80.50	2	T1
2	Indiana	12	964	80.33	2	4
3	Detroit	13	1,040	80.00	3	13
4	Sacramento	13	1,039	79.92	3	T10
5	Utah	14	1,116	79.71	3	16
6	L.A. Lakers	13	1,035	79.62	1	1
7	Boston	14	1,114.5	79.61	3	19
8	Milwaukee	13	1,034	79.54	1	5
9	Philadelphia	12	954	79.50	1	21
9	Portland	12	954	79.50	1	12
11	Cleveland	13	1,033	79.46	2	3
12	Dallas	12	953	79.42	2	6
13	Golden State	14	1,111	79.36	3	7
14	Chicago	12	952	79.33	2	T7
15	New Jersey	14	1,110	79.29	1	17
16	Houston	14	1,109	79.21	2	14
17	L.A. Clippers	13	1,027	79.00	1	24
18	Orlando	13	1,027	79.00	0	18
19	Washington	13	1,027	79.00	0	9
20	Phoenix	15	1,181.5	78.77	0	26
21	Seattle	13	1,023	78.69	1	20
22	New York	14	1,100.5	78.61	2	T10
23	Miami	14	1,099	78.50	1	25
24	Minnesota	12	942	78.50	2	15
25	Charlotte	12	935	77.92	0	23
26	Atlanta	13	1,012	77.85	3	22
27	Denver	15	1,164	77.60	1	27
	East	**169**	**13,375**	**79.14**	**21**	
	West	**185**	**14,647.5**	**79.18**	**22**	
	NBA Average	**354**	**28,022.5**	**79.16**	**43**	
	Atlantic	**81**	**6,405**	**79.07**	**8**	
	Central	**88**	**6,970**	**79.20**	**13**	
	Midwest	**92**	**7,277**	**79.10**	**12**	
	Pacific	**93**	**7,370.5**	**79.25**	**10**	

WEIGHT

Rank	Team	Players	Total Pounds	Average Weight	250+ Pounds	1989 Rank
1	Milwaukee	13	2,970	228.46	2	8
2	Utah	14	3,163	225.93	4	2
3	Detroit	13	2,925	225.00	2	3
4	Sacramento	13	2,880	221.54	5	26
5	Golden State	14	3,100	221.43	1	14
6	Dallas	12	2,632	219.33	2	1
6	Philadelphia	12	2,632	219.33	3	11
8	Houston	14	3,067	219.07	4	9
9	Portland	12	2,622	218.50	1	5
10	L.A. Clippers	13	2,838	218.31	2	12
11	Phoenix	15	3,272	218.13	1	23
12	L.A. Lakers	13	2,832	217.85	1	7
13	Orlando	13	2,822	217.08	1	13
14	San Antonio	12	2,601	216.75	1	17
15	Charlotte	12	2,588	215.67	3	16
16	Cleveland	13	2,785	214.23	1	4
17	Indiana	12	2,570	214.17	2	15
18	Minnesota	12	2,563	213.58	2	22
19	New Jersey	14	2,988	213.43	0	T18
20	Boston	14	2,984	213.14	2	21
21	New York	14	2,962	211.57	0	20
22	Seattle	13	2,749	211.46	1	24
23	Chicago	12	2,528	210.67	0	10
24	Atlanta	13	2,735	210.38	2	27
25	Washington	13	2,725	209.62	0	T5
26	Miami	14	2,920	208.57	1	T18
26	Denver	15	3,069	204.60	1	25
	East	**169**	**36,312**	**214.86**	**18**	
	West	**185**	**40,210**	**217.35**	**27**	
	NBA Average	**354**	**76,522**	**216.16**	**45**	
	Atlantic	**81**	**17,211**	**212.48**	**6**	
	Central	**88**	**19,101**	**217.06**	**12**	
	Midwest	**92**	**19,917**	**216.49**	**15**	
	Pacific	**93**	**20,293**	**218.20**	**12**	

AGE

Rank	Team	Players	Total Years	Avg. Age	30 or Older	1989 Rank
1	Dallas	12	358.84	29.90	6	2
2	Detroit	13	387.30	29.79	6	1
3	L.A. Lakers	13	368.38	28.34	5	3
4	Milwaukee	13	365.37	28.11	5	7
5	Atlanta	13	364.22	28.02	3	8
6	Philadelphia	12	335.76	27.98	4	9
7	Boston	14	389.27	27.80	4	6
8	Portland	12	333.19	27.77	3	12
9	Denver	15	410.29	27.35	4	4
10	New York	14	382.05	27.29	3	20
11	Utah	14	379.69	27.12	2	11
12	Houston	14	379.16	27.08	3	5
13	Golden State	14	376.81	26.91	3	10
14	Seattle	13	349.72	26.90	2	24
15	Indiana	12	322.23	26.85	3	14
16	Phoenix	15	402.19	26.81	4	26
17	Chicago	12	321.44	26.79	3	16
18	Orlando	13	345.90	26.61	1	13
19	Sacramento	13	342.05	26.31	2	23
20	San Antonio	12	315.13	26.26	2	21
21	Minnesota	12	314.58	26.22	2	22
22	New Jersey	14	366.85	26.20	2	18
23	Washington	13	337.50	25.96	2	19
24	Cleveland	13	332.75	25.60	1	17
25	L.A. Clippers	13	331.66	25.512	1	27
26	Charlotte	12	306.14	25.511	1	15
27	Miami	14	344.02	24.57	0	25
	East	**169**	**4,554.89**	**26.95**	**37**	
	West	**185**	**5,007.59**	**27.07**	**40**	
	NBA Average	**354**	**9,562.48**	**27.01**	**77**	
	Atlantic	**81**	**2,155.45**	**26.61**	**15**	
	Central	**88**	**2,399.44**	**27.27**	**22**	
	Midwest	**92**	**2,503.59**	**27.21**	**20**	
	Pacific	**93**	**2,504.00**	**26.92**	**20**	

PRO EXPERIENCE

Rank	Team	Players	Total Years	Avg. Exp.	Rookies	10-Yr Vet.	1989 Rank
1	Dallas	12	87	7.25	0	3	2
2	Detroit	13	89	6.85	2	4	1
3	L.A. Lakers	13	72	5.54	3	2	4
4	Atlanta	13	68	5.23	3	2	7
4	Milwaukee	13	68	5.23	1	1	8
6	Portland	12	62	5.17	1	1	11
7	Philadelphia	12	60	5.00	2	3	9
8	New York	14	66	4.71	1	2	16
9	Seattle	13	59	4.54	1	1	23
10	Boston	14	63	4.50	2	3	3
11	Chicago	12	53	4.42	1	1	15
12	Denver	15	66	4.40	3	3	5
13	Indiana	12	50	4.17	1	0	9
14	Houston	14	54	3.86	3	2	6
15	Phoenix	15	56	3.73	3	0	25
16	Orlando	13	48	3.69	1	0	12
16	Sacramento	13	48	3.69	5	1	22
18	San Antonio	12	44	3.67	3	1	T17
19	Golden State	14	50	3.57	3	0	12
19	Utah	14	50	3.57	4	1	19
21	Washington	13	40	3.08	3	1	T17
22	New Jersey	14	42	3.00	4	1	21
23	Charlotte	12	35	2.92	2	0	14
24	Cleveland	13	35	2.69	3	0	20
25	L.A. Clippers	13	31	2.38	2	0	27
26	Minnesota	12	28	2.33	3	0	26
27	Miami	14	21	1.50	5	0	24
	East	**169**	**690**	**4.08**	**30**	**18**	
	West	**185**	**755**	**4.08**	**35**	**15**	
	NBA Average	**354**	**1,445**	**4.08**	**65**	**33**	
	Atlantic	**81**	**292**	**3.60**	**17**	**10**	
	Central	**88**	**398**	**4.52**	**13**	**8**	
	Midwest	**92**	**377**	**4.10**	**17**	**10**	
	Pacific	**93**	**378**	**4.06**	**18**	**5**	

Two-Way Finalists

I've been spending a lot of time poring over the record books doing the research for this "epic," and I've come up with a couple of categories that should turn you trivia buffs on. If you aren't a trivia buff, but you are a basketball fan, you should get a kick out of this stuff anyway. In the long history of the NBA, there have been only 15 guys (including me) who have been involved in the NBA Finals both as players and coaches. For the record, here's a complete list:

Player/Coach	Team Played For:	Team Coached:
Al Attles	San Francisco '64	Golden State '75
Al Cervi	Syracuse '50	Syracuse '50, '54, '55
Larry Costello	Philadelphia '67	Milwaukee '71
Bill Cunningham	Philadelphia '67	Philadelphia '80, '82, '83
Mike Dunleavy	Houston '81	L.A. Lakers '91
Alex Hannum	Syracuse '50	St. Louis '57, '58
		San Francisco '64
		Philadelphia '67
Tom Heinsohn	Boston '57–65	Boston '74, '76
Red Holzman	Rochester '51	New York '70, '72, '73
Phil Jackson	New York '70, '72, '73	Chicago '91
K.C. Jones	Boston '59–66	Boston '84–87
Ed Macauley	St. Louis '57, '58	St. Louis '60
Pat Riley	L.A. Lakers '72, '73	L.A. '82–85, '87, '88, '89
Bill Russell	Boston '57–66, '68, '69	Boston '68, '69
George Senesky	Philadelphia '47, '48	Philadelphia '56
Paul Seymour	Baltimore '48	St. Louis '61
	Syracuse '50, '54, '55	
Bill Sharman	Boston '57–61	San Francisco '67
		L.A. Lakers '71, '72

Red's Personal List

I get a little satisfaction out of being on that NBA Finals list both as a player and a coach. But I get even more satisfaction out of having the all-time record for coaching the most years in the NBA. My basketball career began in 1945 with Rochester and spanned five decades. I began coaching in 1953 with the Milwaukee Hawks and finished up as the Knicks coach in 1982. That's eighteen seasons, 696 wins. I always wanted to make it 700 wins, but some of my friends tell me that I'm lucky I got the 696. Maybe they're right. Once I was the second all-time winningest coach in NBA history. But as the years have gone on, I fall further and further back in the pack. I also believe I've coached more Rookies of the Year than any other guy. For the record, they were Bob Pettit, Walt Bellamy, Willis Reed, Bob McAdoo, Jerry Lucas, and Earl Monroe.

P.S. My exposure to the NBA Finals is also worth listing. I'm sure you'll write to me if I'm wrong, but I think my record as a player in the Finals ('51), as a coach ('70–72–73), and as a general manager ('70–72–73) stands by itself as something no one else ever did. The only other guys I can think of are Red Auerbach and Bill Sharman, but it wasn't the same for those guys. Auerbach never played, and Bill Sharman wasn't coach and GM at the same time.

William (Red) Holzman's NBA Career

Born August 10, 1920   Height: 5'10"   Weight: 175
College: Baltimore/CCNY

As a player:

Season/Team	Games	FGA	FGM	Pct	FTA	FTM	Pct	Reb	Ast	PF	Pts	Avg
45–46 Rochester (NBL)	34	—	143	—	115	77	.670	—	—	54	363	10.7
46–47 Rochester (NBL)	44	—	227	—	139	74	.532	—	—	68	528	12.0
47–48 Rochester (NBL)	60	—	246	—	182	117	.643	—	—	58	609	10.2
48–49 Rochester	60	691	225	.326	157	96	.611	—	149	93	546	9.1
49–50 Rochester	68	625	206	.330	210	144	.686	—	200	67	556	8.2
50–51 Rochester	68	561	183	.326	179	130	.726	152	147	94	496	7.3
51–52 Rochester	65	372	104	.280	85	61	.718	106	115	95	269	4.1
52–53 Rochester	46	149	38	.255	38	27	.711	40	35	56	103	2.2
53–54 Milwaukee	51	224	74	.330	73	48	.658	46	75	73	196	3.8
Reg. NBA Totals	358	2622	830	.317	742	506	.682	344	721	478	2166	6.1
Reg. NBL Totals	138	—	616	—	436	268	.615	—	—	180	1500	10.9
NBA Playoff Totals	28	145	56	.386	52	31	.596	26	36	27	143	5.1

As a coach:

Season/Team	Regular Season		Playoffs	
	W	L	W	L
53–54 Milwaukee*	10	16	—	—
54–55 Milwaukee	26	46	—	—
55–56 St. Louis	33	39	4	4
56–57 St. Louis**	14	19	—	—
67–68 NY Knicks***	28	17	2	4
68–69 NY Knicks	54	28	6	4
69–70 NY Knicks	60	22	12	7
70–71 NY Knicks	52	30	7	5
71–72 NY Knicks	48	34	9	7
72–73 NY Knicks	57	25	12	5
73–74 NY Knicks	49	33	5	7
74–75 NY Knicks	40	42	1	2
75–76 NY Knicks	38	44	—	—
76–77 NY Knicks	40	42	—	—
78–79 NY Knicks****	25	43	—	—
79–80 NY Knicks	39	43	—	—
80–81 NY Knicks	50	32	0	2
81–82 NY Knicks	33	49	—	—
NBA Totals/18 Years	696	604	58	42

* Replaced Fuzzy Levane (11-35)
** Replaced by Slater Martin (5-3), who was replaced by Alex Hannum (15-16)
*** Replaced Dick McGuire (15-22)
**** Replaced Willis Reed (6-8)

ABOUT THE AUTHORS

William "Red" Holzman was an all-American basketball player at City College before a World War II stint in the Navy. He turned pro with the old Rochester Royals and Milwaukee Hawks of the NBA. He joined the New York Knicks as chief scout and assistant coach in 1957 and scouted such future stars as Walt Frazier, Willis Reed, Bill Bradley, and Cazzie Russell. He became head coach in 1967 and led the Knicks to their only two NBA championships in 1970 and 1973. Red is now a consultant to the Knicks organization, and was inducted into the Basketball Hall of Fame in 1986.

Harvey Frommer is the author of 30 sports books and more than 600 articles. His autobiographical collaborations include: *Red on Red* (Red Holzman), *Throwing Heat* (Nolan Ryan), *Running Tough* (Tony Dorsett), and *Behind the Lines* (Don Strock). He has three children, and lives in North Woodmere, New York, with his wife, Myrna. He is professor of English at the City University of New York.

Index